mezze
MODERN

mezze
MODERN

Delicious Appetizers from Greece, Lebanon, and Turkey

Maria Khalifé
Photography by Stuart West

Interlink Books

An imprint of Interlink Publishing Group, Inc.
Northampton, Massachusetts

First published in 2008 by

INTERLINK BOOKS

An imprint of Interlink Publishing Group, Inc.

46 Crosby Street

Northampton, Massachusetts 01060

www.interlinkbooks.com

1 3 5 7 9 10 8 6 4 2

ISBN   978-1-56656-713-8

Senior Editor: Corinne Masciocchi

Design: Pascal Thivillon

Jacket design: Juliana Spear

Photography: Stuart West

Food styling: Stella Murphy

Editorial Direction: Rosemary Wilkinson

Production: Hema Gohil and Lynne Saner

Reproduction by Colour Scan Overseas, Singapore

Printed and bound by Times Offset (M) Bhd Sdn, Malaysia

Contents

Introduction

The history of mezze is steeped in the Greek, Turkish, and Middle Eastern cultures, and is something I feel very passionate about, having grown up with mezze as an integral part of my family's meals.

The concept of mezze came about a few centuries ago when the men arrived home in the late afternoon after a hard day's work. They would sit outside their houses enjoying small tasty dishes accompanied by a drink while socializing with friends and neighbors. The dishes were always pre-prepared, allowing wives the time to spend indoors preparing the main evening meal.

This way of sharing food and drink without any ceremony or service was a form of bonding enjoyed by cultures in bygone times, and to my great delight mezze continues to grow in popularity with today's generation and I hope generations to come.

I had the pleasure, while researching the many delicious recipes for this book, to meet with my good friend, Andonis Panayotopoulos, the Chairman of the Greek Academy of Taste. He proved to be a wonderful source of inspiration for the Greek selection of recipes and is a committed supporter of mezze. In fact, at all official functions the academy serves between eight and 10 dishes with three to four distillates so the group can enjoy socializing before the main meal is served.

I also had expert advice on Turkish dishes from my good friends Hasan Açanal and Guzin Yalin, both experts in food communications and board members at the Conservatoire International des Cuisines Mediterranéennes.

Traditionally, a variety of mezze dishes is served with a drink before the main meal, offering friends and family the opportunity to socialize and unwind after a busy day. Featuring over 90 recipes, I'm sure you will enjoy selecting from the book a wonderful array of dishes time and again for your friends and family to share. The recipes are divided into four chapters – hot and cold mezze, salads and pastries, along with a glossary of terms – and the majority of ingredients are widely available.

Throughout my years as producer of Soufra Daimeh, a widely broadcast TV food show attracting over one million viewers, magazine editor, and author of the best-selling and award-winning *Middle Eastern Cookbook*, I have been blessed with a passion to discover the most delicious recipes in this region. As you can imagine it was a delight to work on this book, selecting dishes from across Greece, Turkey, and Lebanon which are as loved today as they were centuries ago.

I hope you'll enjoy discovering the rich variety of tastes and textures within these pages that have been lovingly selected for your enjoyment.

Bon appetit, or as we like to say in Lebanon, soufra daimeh!

Glossary

In this section you will find an A to Z guide to some of the most commonly featured herbs, spices, meats, vegetables, dairy products, and legumes, along with tips on how to cook them and which dishes they complement.

Basil Large, fleshy leaves, particularly popular in Italian dishes such as pesto, basil marries well with tomatoes. To preserve the bright green or purple color of the leaves, do not chop the leaves with a knife, but tear by hand. Use the leaves only. The purple variety has a stronger taste so less is needed.

Beet In past times, beet was cultivated for its leaves only, but these days the bulb, with its high sugar content, is the more valuable part. The most famous usage is in borscht, although beet is frequently used as a vegetable and in salads. Cook without trimming, so the color does not "bleed."

Bulgur/Burghul Wheat grains which are hulled and steamed before cracking, then dried. Popular in Middle Eastern cuisine, especially vegetarian dishes, such as tabouleh.

Cabbage Related to broccoli, cauliflower, kohlrabi, and Brussels sprouts. Choose heads which are heavy for their size, with crisp, shiny outer leaves. Eat raw in salads or cook for a minimum time in a covered saucepan and drain well.

Chickpeas Also known as ceci and garbanzo beans. Medium-size peas with a small pointed top. Robust and nutty flavored, chickpeas hold their shape well with cooking. Soak chickpeas overnight in water before use, then cook for approximately 1 hour.

Cilantro This leaf has a distinctive aroma. It is used extensively in Mediterranean, Latin American, and Asian cooking. People either love or hate this herb with a passion! The roots and leaves are a must in Thai green curry. Coriander seeds can also be used; these have a lemony flavor when crushed and can also be ground.

Cloves Cloves lose their potency after prolonged storage. To perform a freshness test, drop a clove in cold water – if fresh, it will either sink or float upright, if stale it will lie flat on the surface. Use whole or ground in meat and marinated fish dishes, pastries, and mulled wine.

Cumin Without it, Middle Eastern and Latin American food would be dull. It is a popular flavoring in Indonesian cuisine and is nearly always present in curry powder. Dried cumin is often used in fruit chutneys.

Dandelion (chicory) After discarding the tough stems, the leaves are used as a salad ingredient or cooked as a vegetable side dish. The pleasantly bitter leaves should be briefly blanched before using in a salad or cooked until tender in water.

Dibs el rouman (pomegranate paste) Commonly used as a flavoring in Middle Eastern cooking, this paste is used to enhance both sweet and savory dishes to impart a rich, complex flavor.

Dill Light green and feathery with tiny greeny-yellow flowers. This herb is used in fish and egg dishes, or finely chopped in salads. Especially good with cucumber or cottage cheese.

Dolmades An Arabic term meaning "something stuffed," dolmades are vine (grape) leaf parcels and can be made with a number of different fillings, such as rice, meat, and vegetables.

Dry yeast A leavening agent which produces carbon dioxide by fermenting sugars. Used to make breads and cake rise. Store in a cool, dry, dark place.

Eggplant This smooth-skinned, shiny fruit comes in a variety of colors, including white, green, pink, blue-black, black, and most commonly dark purple. Look for unblemished fruit, which are heavy for their size. Most eggplants do not have bitter juices, but if they do, the fruit can be sliced, sprinkled with salt, and left to stand for 30 minutes to extract them. Rinse and pat them dry.

Fava beans Also known as broad beans, feves, Windsor beans, and horse beans. These are oval-shaped with a thick skin. The nutty flavor and creamy texture make them especially favored in Middle Eastern and Mediterranean cuisines.

Feta cheese A traditional Greek cheese usually made from sheep's milk but can also be made from cow or goat's milk. It has a salty taste and crumbly texture and is a wonderful addition to salads.

Garlic Garlic is used with almost any savory food. Its flavor depends on how it is prepared – cooked garlic being much milder than raw, chopped garlic. It can be used raw or fried, poached, roasted, or sautéed, and can be cooked peeled or unpeeled. Choose a firm, hard head of garlic with no soft or discolored patches. Do not refrigerate but store in a cool, dry place.

Ghee A clarified butter or pure butter fat that can be

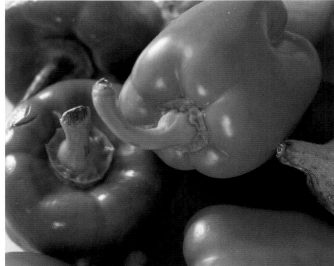

heated to a high temperature without burning. Predominantly used in Indian cooking, ghee has a long shelf life.

Halloumi cheese Traditionally made with sheep or goat's milk but now more often made with cow's milk. Similar to mozzarella, this cheese has a rubbery texture and "squeaks" when eaten. It can be fried or grilled and goes well in salads or as an appetizer.

Kaskaval cheese Traditionally a Bulgarian sheep's milk cheese similar to Greek Kasseri cheese, it also has a strong history in Turkey. A dense cheese with a yellow color and strong, biting taste.

Kasseri cheese A Greek cheese made from goat or sheep's milk with a hard texture and sharp, salty flavor. Good for cooking and grating over hot dishes.

Lentils Flat, lens-shaped legume, red or green to brown in color. High in protein, lentils are full-flavored and are commonly used in soups, stews, and rice dishes. Cooking time varies depending on variety and can take 20, 40, or 60 minutes.

Makanek (sausage) Originating in Lebanon, makanek is a thin sausage made from pork or beef, and spiced with red and black pepper.

Millet A nutritious, easily digestible grain that can be used as a thickener when added to soups. Also used to make bread.

Mint Use fresh sprigs in drinks, and chopped leaves with lamb, vegetables (especially new potatoes and peas), and in fruit salads or to make a mint sauce.

Myzithra cheese Also known as Mitzithra, it is a Greek cheese made of ewe's milk, available both fresh when it is similar to cottage cheese, and aged when it is firm and strong, and is ideal for grating.

Oregano An aromatic herb frequently used in Italian cooking, it can be used fresh or dried and goes well in tomato-based sauces and for seasoning meat.

Paprika Varying from mild to strong, this spice is mainly used to add flavor and color to cooking and is made from drying sweet red peppers and then grinding them into a rich, red powder. Great in stews and vegetable dishes.

Parsley Probably the most familiar variety of culinary herb, it is hardy and highly nutritious. There are two types: curly-leaf parsley has bright green, tightly-curled leaves and is used primarily as a garnish; flat-leaf parsley has a stronger flavor and is preferred for cooking.

Finely chopped parsley leaves are amongst the mix in "fines herbes" and the stalks are used in bouquet garni.

Pine nuts Also known as pine kernels, these are the edible seeds from pine trees. Oily and rich in protein, they are used in savory dishes and should be kept refrigerated.

Pita bread A versatile flat bread that can be split in half to create a pocket. It is very popular in Turkey, Greece, and the Middle East, and is especially good with dips or stuffed with various fillings.

Soujouk (hot sausage) A large sausage made with minced pork or beef and pancetta popular from the Balkans to the Middle East. Some sausages are highly spiced and others seasoned with herbs and garlic.

Sumac The dried berries of this Mediterranean shrub are ground into a reddish-purplish powder. Available in local Lebanese and Middle Eastern food stores, sumac is used to infuse a dish with lemon flavor, without adding any liquid and is sprinkled on fattoush.

Swiss chard Sometimes confused with spinach, it is also known as silver beet. The leaves should be dark green and shiny and the stems white, without signs of bruising. Use the leaves cooked as you would spinach,

or raw, mixed with other salad greens. Use the stems in soups or stews, or braise them until tender, then bake in a gratin dish with Parmesan cheese.

Tahini Made from ground sesame seeds, tahini is a smooth paste with a high calcium content, particularly when the seeds have not been crushed. It is used commonly in Middle Eastern cuisines. Use in salads, hummus, and baba ganoush, and also as a sauce or in cakes.

Thyme A versatile herb, it has strong, aromatic leaves that are used in soups, stews, bean dishes or meat of any kind, including terrines and pâtés. Also good with vegetables, particularly roast potatoes.

Yogurt Made from either cow's or sheep's milk, it can contain living bacteria and must be refrigerated and consumed by the "use by" date. Available in a number of styles, it can contain up to 10.5 percent fat.

Za'atar A group of herbs and a Middle Eastern spice blend containing sumac, sesame, and marjoram. These fresh herbs are available only around the Mediterranean. Local Lebanese and Middle Eastern shops sell the spice blend, which is sprinkled on dishes including meats, vegetables, and cheeses before baking. Good with barbecued meat.

Cold mezze

Eggplants stuffed with vegetables

Batinjan mahchi bil khoudar

SERVES 5
COOKING TIME: 1 HOUR 15 MINUTES

2 lb 3 oz short, thin eggplants
¾ cup water
1½ Tbsp tomato paste
Pinch of salt

For the stuffing
Bunch of parsley, finely chopped
⅓ cup olive oil
4 large tomatoes, cubed
¼ cup lemon juice
5½ oz small-grain white rice
2 small onions, peeled and chopped
Pinch of salt and white pepper

1 Cut the tops off the eggplants and discard them. Carefully scoop out the flesh without breaking the skin, leaving a ¼ in thickness of flesh all round. Be careful not to cut through the end. Rinse and drain.

2 Prepare the stuffing by combining all the stuffing ingredients in a large bowl. Fill the eggplant hollows to three-quarters full with the stuffing, leaving enough space at the top for the rice to expand. Sprinkle the top of the eggplants with salt.

3 Arrange the eggplants horizontally in a large saucepan, cover with the water, then press with a slightly smaller saucepan lid that fits inside the saucepan. Then cover with the pan's lid and bring to a boil over high heat. Reduce heat and cook gently for approximately 45 minutes, until the eggplants are almost tender.

4 Dissolve the tomato paste in 1 cup water and add to the saucepan. Bring to a boil again until the eggplants are tender. Remove from heat and set aside to cool. Serve cold.

Bulgur pilaf

Bulgur pilavi

SERVES 8
COOKING TIME: 30 MINUTES

1 lb 2 oz coarse bulgur
3½ oz butter
2 medium onions, peeled and finely chopped
3 large tomatoes, peeled, seeded, and diced
2 small sweet green peppers, seeded
  and finely chopped
1 tsp salt
Pinch of freshly ground black pepper
2½ cups meat stock

1 Rinse the bulgur in plenty of water and drain.

2 Melt the butter in a saucepan, fry the onions until soft, then add the bulgur and stir over medium heat for about 5 minutes. Add the tomatoes, peppers, salt, and pepper, and stir well. Remove from heat.

3 In a separate pan, bring the meat stock to a boil, then add it to the bulgur mixture. Stir and cover, bring to a boil, then cook on low heat until the liquid has evaporated.

4 Remove from heat, cover with a dry kitchen cloth, and replace the lid. Allow to stand for 10 minutes, stir thoroughly, and let stand for another 5 minutes. Pour into a serving dish and serve cold.

Stuffed grape leaves

Dolmades

SERVES 6
COOKING TIME: 1 HOUR

14 oz fresh grape leaves
Juice of 1 lemon

For the filling
3 artichoke hearts, grated
2 potatoes, peeled and grated
3 zucchinis, grated
3 onions, peeled and grated
1 lb 2 oz white rice
Small bunch of parsley, finely chopped
Small bunch of fresh mint, finely chopped
1 cup olive oil
1 tsp salt
1 tsp freshly ground black pepper

1　Blanch the grape leaves in a bowl of hot water for 5 minutes, then remove from heat, strain, and separate them.

2　In a separate bowl, mix together the filling ingredients.

3　Place a teaspoon of the filling into the center of each grape leaf, then fold the leaf over to make a parcel. Repeat with all the mixture and grape leaves.

4　Place the grape leaf parcels in a pan, cover with hot water, then cover and simmer gently for approximately 1 hour.

5　Once cooked, remove the dolmades from the pan with a slotted spoon, arrange on a serving dish, and pour the lemon juice over them. Serve cold.

Pilaf with eggplants

Zeytinyagli patlicanli pilav

SERVES 10
COOKING TIME: 30 MINUTES

8 long, thin eggplants
1 lb 9 oz arborio rice
2 tsp salt
2 tsp super fine sugar
2 Tbsp sunflower oil
4 cups olive oil
7 medium onions, peeled and finely chopped
5 mild green chilies, finely chopped
2 tomatoes peeled, seeded, and diced
4 cups water
1 tsp allspice
Sprig of dill, finely chopped
Sprig of fresh mint, finely chopped

1 Rinse and partially peel the eggplants in alternate lengthwise strips. Remove and discard the stalks and cut the eggplants into small cubes. Soak in salted water for about 20 minutes to remove any bitter juices.

2 Place the rice in a bowl, cover with hot water, and stir in 1 tablespoon of salt. Let stand for 10 minutes, then rinse thoroughly and drain.

3 Remove the eggplants from the water, squeeze gently, and pat dry with paper towels. Sprinkle 1 teaspoon of salt and sugar over the eggplant cubes and rub in well. Fry the cubes in the sunflower oil until golden brown, then drain on paper towels.

4 Heat the olive oil in a pan and fry the onions, chilies, and tomatoes until lightly cooked, then stir in the water and the remaining teaspoons of salt and sugar and the allspice. Bring to a boil and stir in the rice. Cover and bring to a boil, then lower heat and cook gently until the rice has absorbed the liquid.

5 Sprinkle the dill and mint over the rice and lay the eggplants over the top. Cover and cook for 5 minutes on low heat, then remove from heat and stand for 20 minutes. Stir the rice, cover, and stand for a further 2 minutes. Transfer to a serving dish and serve cold.

Dried beans with tomato and spinach

Fasolia xera yachnista

SERVES 6
COOKING TIME: 1 HOUR 15 MINUTES

1 lb 2 oz dried mixed beans (to include
  fava, kidney, and pinto beans)
½ cup olive oil
1 onion, peeled and finely chopped
Small bunch of dill, finely chopped
1 lb 2 oz tomatoes, finely chopped
1 tsp salt
1 tsp freshly ground black pepper
2¾ cups water
2 lb 3 oz spinach, finely chopped

1 Place the beans in a large pot and cover well with salted water. Boil for 30 minutes, then drain.

2 Heat the olive oil in a pan and fry the onion and dill for 10 minutes.

3 Add the beans and tomatoes to the pan, along with the salt, pepper, and water. Simmer for 10 minutes until almost cooked. Add the spinach and simmer for another 15 minutes. Remove from heat, allow to cool, and serve cold.

LEBANON

Potatoes in oil and lemon dressing

Batata bil zeit wal hamoud

SERVES 4
COOKING TIME: 25 MINUTES

2 lb 3 oz new potatoes, unpeeled
2 garlic cloves, peeled and crushed
¼ cup lemon juice
⅓ cup olive oil
Pinch of salt and white pepper
3½ oz fresh parsley, chopped, to garnish

1 Rinse the potatoes and boil whole in a saucepan of boiling, salted water until cooked. Remove from heat, drain, and leave to cool. Peel the potatoes and cut into medium cubes, then transfer to a serving dish.

2 In a bowl, mix the garlic with the lemon juice and olive oil. Season with salt and white pepper. Add the sauce to the potato cubes and mix well. Sprinkle with parsley and serve cold.

Fish filet in tahini sauce

Tajin el samak

SERVES 6
COOKING TIME: 30 MINUTES

2 lb 3 oz sea bass filets, sliced
¼ cup olive oil
2 onions, peeled and sliced
7 oz tahini
¾ cup water
⅓ cup lemon juice
1 tsp salt
Pinch of white pepper
1 tsp cumin
½ tsp Tabasco sauce
2 oz walnuts, crushed
2 oz pine nuts, toasted
Vegetable oil, for frying
4 pita pockets
1 lemon, cut into wedges, to garnish
Fresh parsley leaves, to garnish

1 Arrange the fish filets in an oven tray. Bake for 15 minutes then leave to cool.

2 Heat the olive oil in a small pan and fry the onions until golden brown. Add in the tahini, water, lemon juice, salt, pepper, cumin, Tabasco, and walnuts. Cook the mixture until it thickens to a paste-like consistency. Pour over the fish filets and sprinkle with pine nuts.

3 Fry the bread in the vegetable oil. Drain over paper towels, then arrange around a serving platter with the fish in the center. Garnish with the lemon wedges and parsley.

Fava beans in lemon, olive oil, and garlic

Fasulye aridah moutabaleh

SERVES 5
COOKING TIME: 1 HOUR 15 MINUTES

12½ oz fava beans, soaked in water
   for 10 hours or overnight
⅓ cup olive oil

For the dressing
3 garlic cloves, peeled and crushed
¼ cup lemon juice
Pinch of salt

1 Rinse the pre-soaked fava beans, drain, and transfer to a pan. Cover with cold water and cook over high heat for about 1 hour, until tender. Transfer to a serving dish and allow to cool.

2 To prepare the dressing, mix the garlic with the lemon juice and salt. Pour over the fava beans and drizzle the olive oil on top.

 TURKEY

Beet dip

Yogurtlu pancar mezesi

SERVES 8–10

3 beets
Juice of ½ lemon
1 garlic clove, peeled and crushed
5 Tbsp Greek yogurt
Pinch of salt
1 Tbsp olive oil
Pita bread, to serve

1 Boil the beets for approximately 15 minutes, or until cooked, or microwave with 2 tablespoons of water for 4 minutes.

2 Place the beets, lemon juice, and garlic in a blender and blend together until smooth. Add the yogurt and salt, and blend again until smooth.

3 Transfer to a serving dish, drizzle with the olive oil, and serve with hot pita breads.

Grape leaves with rice stuffing

Zeytinyagli yaprak dolmasi

SERVES 10
COOKING TIME: 1 HOUR 40 MINUTES

For the stuffing
4½ oz white rice
2 Tbsp currants
⅓ cup olive oil
⅓ cup sunflower oil
2 Tbsp pine nuts
6 medium onions, peeled and finely chopped
1 tsp cinnamon
1 tsp allspice
1 tsp white pepper
1 tsp salt
⅓ cup hot water
½ bunch of fresh mint, chopped
Bunch of dill, chopped

14 oz fresh grape leaves
⅓ cup olive oil
1 tsp super fine sugar
10 cups cold water
1 lemon, peeled and sliced

1 Prepare the stuffing by soaking the rice in cold water for 30 minutes, then rinsing thoroughly and draining. Soak the currants in warm water for about 15 minutes until they swell.

2 In a frying pan, heat the olive and sunflower oils, then add the pine nuts and onions, and brown slightly. Add the soaked rice and cook for 10 minutes. Then add the soaked currants, spices, salt, and hot water, and cook over low heat for 15 minutes, until the water has evaporated. Remove from heat, then stir in the mint and dill and set aside to cool.

3 Scald the grape leaves in boiling water, then dip in cold water to preserve their color. If the leaves are preserved in brine, soak them in warm water and rinse thoroughly to remove the excess salt.

4 Open each leaf with the glossy side facing down and veins facing upwards. Place a teaspoon of the rice filling at the base of each leaf and fold the edges inwards over the stuffing, then roll up to form a finger-sized dolma. Repeat until all the mixture is finished. There should be about 30 dolmas in total. Place any discarded coarse leaves at the bottom of a saucepan. Layer the stuffed grape leaves over them with the folded edges facing down.

5 In a small bowl, mix the olive oil and sugar together and pour over the vine leaves. Pour over the water. Arrange the lemon slices on top and a damp sheet of greaseproof paper over this, weighted down with a plate. Cover and bring to a boil over high heat, then simmer for approximately 45 minutes. When most of the water has evaporated and the grape leaves are tender, set aside to cool with the lid on.

Green beans

Zeytinyagli taze fasulye

SERVES 10
COOKING TIME: 1 HOUR

3 lb 5 oz runner beans or green beans
2 medium tomatoes
½ cup olive oil
½ tsp tomato paste
2 large onions, peeled
1 tsp salt
3 tsp super fine sugar
4 cups water

1   Rinse the beans, then top and tail them.

2   Peel, seed, and dice the tomatoes, then lightly fry in the olive oil with the tomato paste until it forms a purée.

3   Arrange the beans in neat layers in a broad pan. Place the whole peeled onions on top. Strain the tomato purée and pour over.

4   Add the salt, sugar, and water, and cover with a circle of damp waxed paper weighted down with a plate. Bring to a boil on high heat, then cook over low heat for approximately 1 hour, or until most of the liquid has evaporated and the beans are tender. Set aside to cool.

5   Drain the liquid into a bowl, remove and discard the onions, and turn the beans upside down into a serving dish. Pour the liquid over and serve cold.

Mixed bean salad

Palikaria

SERVES 4
COOKING TIME: 45 MINUTES

3½ oz dried mixed beans
   (to include kidney, pinto, and fava beans)
3½ oz millet
3½ oz bulgur (cracked wheat)
3½ oz dried chickpeas
3½ oz dried lentils
3½ oz frozen peas
1 tsp salt
1 tsp freshly ground black pepper
2 spring onions, finely chopped
1 Tbsp dill, finely chopped
½ cup olive oil
2 Tbsp lemon juice

1   Soak all the legumes, except for the lentils and peas, in water overnight. Soak the bulgur and chickpeas separately to allow for more time cooking.

2   The following day, drain the bulgur and chickpeas and place in a pan with plenty of water and boil for 30 minutes.

3   Then add the remaining soaked and drained legumes, along with the lentils and peas, and boil for about 15 minutes until they are soft. Drain and place in a serving bowl, and season with salt and pepper.

4   In a bowl, mix together the spring onions, dill, olive oil, and lemon juice, then drizzle over the salad. Serve cold.

 GREECE

Fish roe dip

Taramosalata

SERVES 4
COOKING TIME: 30 MINUTES

1 large potato, peeled and cut into ½ in cubes
4 oz codfish roe
½ onion, peeled and minced
3 Tbsp fresh lemon juice
½ cup olive oil
1 black olive, to garnish
Warm pita bread, to serve

1   Place the potato cubes in a saucepan and cover with water. Bring to a boil, then reduce heat and simmer until cooked through. Drain and set aside to cool.

2   Transfer the potato pieces to a bowl, along with the roe, onion, and lemon juice, and blend until smooth.

3   Add the olive oil and blend to a smooth, creamy consistency. Transfer to a serving bowl, garnish with the olive, and refrigerate until cold. Serve with warm pita bread.

Hot chili tahini dip

Tarator har

SERVES 4

1 garlic clove, peeled
Pinch salt
Juice of 1 lemon
¾ oz tahini
¼ cup water
Pinch of hot paprika
1 green chili, seeded and chopped
Warm bread, to serve

1 In a bowl, crush the garlic with the salt. Mix in the lemon juice and tahini.

2 Gradually mix in the water until the dip is smooth. Stir in the hot paprika and chopped pepper. Transfer to a serving dish. Serve with warm bread.

 TURKEY

Swooning imam

Imam bayildi

SERVES 10
COOKING TIME: 1 HOUR 30 MINUTES

10 medium eggplants
Sunflower oil, for frying
¾ cup olive oil
6 medium onions, peeled and finely chopped
6 large tomatoes, peeled, seeded, and diced
6 garlic cloves, peeled and crushed
Bunch of parsley, chopped
1 tsp salt
1 Tbsp super fine sugar
1¾ cups water
Juice of 1 lemon

1 Rinse the eggplants, remove the stalks, and partially peel the eggplants in alternate strips. Fry the eggplants whole in sunflower oil until golden brown, then split open lengthwise leaving both ends uncut.

2 Place the eggplants in a shallow saucepan side by side in a single layer with the open sides facing up and set aside.

3 Heat half the olive oil in a pan and fry the onions until lightly browned. Add the tomatoes, garlic, parsley, and salt and simmer for 15 minutes. Remove the mixture from the heat and stuff the eggplants with it.

4 In a bowl, mix together the sugar, water, lemon juice, and the remaining olive oil and pour over the eggplants. Cover and cook on medium heat for 1 hour or until tender. Transfer to a serving platter and serve cold.

Stuffed cabbage leaves

Lahanodolmades

SERVES 6
COOKING TIME: 1 HOUR 30 MINUTES

1 large cabbage, rinsed and separated into leaves
2 Tbsp olive oil

For the filling
Small fennel bulb, finely chopped
Small bunch of parsley, finely chopped
Small bunch of fresh mint, finely chopped
4 tomatoes, grated
3 onions, peeled and grated
1 lb 2 oz white rice
1 tsp salt
1 tsp freshly ground black pepper

1 Blanch the cabbage leaves in a bowl of hot water for 5 minutes, then remove from the water and separate them. In a large bowl mix together the filling ingredients.

2 Place a teaspoon of the filling into the center of each cabbage leaf, then fold the leaf over to make a parcel. Repeat until all the mixture is finished and you have filled approximately 30 dolmades, making sure you set aside about four cabbage leaves. Shred these leaves.

3 Pour the olive oil in a saucepan, then layer the shredded cabbage leaves on the bottom of the pan. Place the dolmades in circles on top of the shredded leaves.

4 Add water to cover the parcels and 2 tablespoons of olive oil and simmer until the water is absorbed. While cooking, occasionally gently shake the pot to stop the lower cabbage leaves from sticking to the bottom of the pan. When cooked, remove from the pan, allow to cool, and serve cold.

Eggplants with tomatoes

Batinjan bil banadoora

SERVES 6
COOKING TIME: 1 HOUR 15 MINUTES

6 long, thin eggplants
⅔ cup olive oil
Juice of ½ lemon
¾ cup water

For the stuffing
3 medium onions, peeled and finely chopped
3 large peeled tomatoes, seeded and chopped
1 Tbsp salt
1 Tbsp super fine sugar
1 large garlic clove, peeled and crushed
½ bunch of parsley, chopped

1 Start by preparing the eggplants. Cut off the tops and partially peel the eggplants in alternate strips. Make a deep lengthwise score down each eggplant without cutting right to either end. Mix one tablespoon of salt into a large bowl of water and soak the eggplants for 30 minutes.

2 Prepare the stuffing by combining all the stuffing ingredients together. Drain and rinse the eggplants, dry well, and arrange in a shallow saucepan. Fill the splits of eggplants with the stuffing.

3 Pour the olive oil, lemon juice, and water over the eggplants, then press with a slightly smaller saucepan lid that fits inside the saucepan. Then cover with the pan's lid and bring to a boil over high heat. Reduce heat and cook gently for approximately 45 minutes, until the eggplants are tender and the liquid has evaporated.

4 Set aside to cool with the saucepan lid on. Carefully transfer the eggplants to a serving dish and serve cold.

Artichokes with fava beans

Zeytinyagli ic baklali enginar

SERVES 10
COOKING TIME: 1 HOUR

10 artichoke hearts
Juice of 2 lemons
2 tsp salt
7 tsp all-purpose flour
3 medium onions, peeled and chopped
7 ½ cups water
6 tsp super fine sugar
½ cup olive oil

For the fava beans
1 lb 14 oz fava beans
3 large onions, peeled and chopped
4 cups water
1 ¾ cups olive oil
5 tsp sugar
2 tsp salt
3 sprigs of dill, chopped, to garnish

1 Rub the artichoke hearts with the juice of one of the lemons and salt to avoid discoloration, then place the hearts in a pan along with the juice from the remaining lemon, flour, onions, water, sugar, and olive oil.

2 Cover with a sheet of waxed paper pushed down into the saucepan and weighted down with a plate. Cook over gentle heat for 45 minutes.

3 In the meantime prepare the fava beans. Shell them, remove the skin, and place in a pan with the onions, water, olive oil, sugar, and salt. Cook over medium heat for approximately 1 hour, or until beans are tender. Remove from heat and allow to cool.

4 Remove the artichokes from heat and set aside to cool without removing the cover. When cooled, place the artichokes on a serving dish and fill the centers with the fava bean mixture. Cover with the juice from the cooked artichokes and garnish with dill.

GREECE

Yogurt dip

Tzatziki

SERVES 4

2¼ cups strained yogurt
1 cucumber, peeled and finely diced
4 garlic cloves, peeled and crushed
1 Tbsp olive oil
Pinch of salt and freshly ground black pepper
Warm pita bread, to serve

1 Blend the yogurt, cucumber, and garlic in a food processor until smooth.

2 Add the olive oil, salt, and pepper, and blend again. Pour into a serving bowl and refrigerate until chilled. Serve with warm pita bread.

 LEBANON

Fried eggplants with yogurt dip

Batinjan makli ma salsat el laban

SERVES 4
COOKING TIME: 15 MINUTES

2 large eggplants
Salt and white pepper
3½ cups vegetable oil

For the dip
Pinch of salt
1 garlic clove, peeled
1⅓ cups plain yogurt
3 medium cucumbers, cubed
1 Tbsp dried mint

1 Remove the tops of the eggplants and cut into thick rounds. Season with salt and pepper and leave to drain on paper towels.

2 To prepare the dip, crush the salt with the garlic in a bowl. Stir in the yogurt, then mix in the cucumber and mint. Refrigerate until chilled.

3 In the meantime, fry the eggplant rounds in the oil until golden brown. Drain on paper towels and serve with the yogurt dip on the side.

Walnut dip

Mohamra

SERVES 8–10

3 garlic cloves, peeled
3 jalapeño peppers, chopped
6 oz chopped walnuts
1 medium red pepper, seeded and chopped
1 small onion, peeled and finely chopped
2 Tbsp molasses
2 Tbsp olive oil
1 Tbsp ground cumin
Pinch of salt
Hot pita bread, to serve

Blend all the ingredients until the mixture forms a smooth consistency. Place in a serving dish and serve with hot pita bread.

 LEBANON

Swiss chard in tahini dip

Silq bil tahini

SERVES 5
COOKING TIME: 30 MINUTES

1 lb 2 oz Swiss chard, leaves discarded
1 garlic clove, peeled and crushed
Pinch of salt
7 oz tahini
⅓ cup lemon juice
2 Tbsp fresh chopped parsley, to garnish

1 Rinse the Swiss chard stalks and remove any thin fine veins using a sharp kitchen knife. Cut the stalks into 1 in pieces, then transfer to a saucepan and cover with water. Cook over medium heat until tender. Remove from heat and leave to cool. Drain and transfer to a large salad bowl.

2 In a small bowl, mix the garlic with the salt, tahini, lemon juice, and a little water until smooth. Add the mix to Swiss chard stalks and mix well. Sprinkle fresh parsley on top to garnish and serve cold.

Eggplants with rice stuffing

Zeytinyagli patlican dolmasi

SERVES 10
COOKING TIME: 1 HOUR 40 MINUTES

For the stuffing
4½ oz white rice
2 Tbsp currants
⅓ cup olive oil
⅓ cup sunflower oil
2 Tbsp pine nuts
6 medium onions, peeled and finely chopped
1 tsp cinnamon
1 tsp allspice
1 tsp white pepper
1 tsp super fine sugar
1 tsp salt
⅓ cup hot water
½ bunch of fresh mint, chopped
Bunch of dill, chopped

10 medium eggplants
Juice of 1 lemon
⅓ cup olive oil
Pinch of salt and sugar
1 ¾ cup hot water

1 Start by preparing the stuffing. Soak the rice in cold water for 30 minutes, then rinse thoroughly and drain. Soak the currants in a little warm water for about 15 minutes until they swell, then drain. In a frying pan, heat the olive and sunflower oils and fry the pine nuts and onions until lightly browned. Add the rice and cook for 10 minutes. Add the soaked currants, spices, sugar, salt, and hot water, and cook over low heat for 15 minutes until the water has evaporated. Stir in the mint and dill. Set aside to cool.

2 De-stalk and hollow out the eggplants. Keep the cores to one side and cut into ½ in lengths. Place the cored eggplants in a large bowl of water with the lemon juice to prevent discoloration.

3 Preheat the oven to 375° F (190° C). Fill the eggplants with the rice stuffing and plug with the cores fixed in place with toothpicks.

4 Prick the skin of the stuffed eggplants in several places and place in a deep baking tray. In a bowl, mix together the olive oil, salt, and sugar, and pour over eggplants. Pour over the hot water. Place a damp sheet of waxed paper over the eggplants with ends tucked in. Bake for approximately 25 minutes, then set aside to cool.

LEBANON

Beirut-style chickpea dip

Hommus Beiruty

SERVES 4
COOKING TIME: 15 MINUTES

15 oz canned, cooked chickpeas
2 garlic cloves, peeled and crushed
¾ cup water
4 Tbsp tahini
½ cup lemon juice
3 Tbsp fresh parsley, chopped
Pinch of salt
2 Tbsp olive oil
3 Tbsp canned, cooked fava beans

1 In a food processor, blend the chickpeas with the garlic and half the water until smooth.

2 Dissolve the tahini in the lemon juice and remaining water, then blend with the chickpea mixture. The mixture should be thick and smooth. Mix in the fresh parsley and season with salt.

3 Transfer the mixture to small serving dishes and garnish with the olive oil and cooked fava beans.

 TURKEY

Fava bean purée

Fava

SERVES 10
COOKING TIME: 30 MINUTES

1 lb 2 oz dried fava beans
12½ oz fresh fava beans, shelled
4 cups water
1 large onion, peeled and chopped
3 small potatoes, peeled and diced
¾ cup olive oil
2 Tbsp sunflower oil
2 tsp salt
4 tsp super fine sugar
1 Tbsp fresh dill, chopped

1 Rinse the dried beans, place them in a saucepan with the fresh shelled beans, and the water. Add the onion, potatoes, olive and sunflower oils, salt and sugar, and cook over medium heat until the ingredients form a purée.

2 Use an electric blender or press the mixture through a wire strainer to form a smooth, thick purée. Pour into a bowl and leave to cool.

3 If not serving immediately, cover with cling wrap or a damp cloth and place in the refrigerator. When ready to serve, transfer to a serving dish and garnish with the dill.

Circassian chicken

Cerkez tavugu

SERVES 10
COOKING TIME: 45 MINUTES

1 large chicken
3 ½ cups water
1 medium potato, peeled and chopped
1 small onion, peeled and chopped
1 carrot, peeled and chopped
½ tsp salt

For the walnut sauce
14 oz shelled walnuts
2 slices stale white bread, crusts removed
2 tsp ground red peppercorns
2 garlic cloves, peeled and crushed
½ tsp salt

1 Rinse the chicken and place it in a large pan with the water. Add the potato, onion, and carrot, and bring to a boil. When the chicken is partially cooked, add the salt, cover, and continue to boil until the chicken is tender.

2 Remove the chicken, strain off the stock into a separate bowl, separate the bones and skin, and cut the meat into small pieces.

3 To make the sauce, crush the walnuts or pound to a paste in a pestle and mortar, then place in a mixing bowl.

4 Soak the bread in the chicken stock, squeeze out the moisture, and crumble into the walnuts, then mix until smooth. Add the peppercorns, garlic, and salt and knead together. Place the mixture in a piece of muslin and squeeze the moisture out into a bowl.

5 Transfer the muslin mixture to a bowl, then beat in 1 cup of the warm chicken stock until a pouring consistency is achieved.

6 Place the chicken pieces into a serving bowl and pour over the walnut sauce.

Mackerel salad

Uskumru salatasi

SERVES 2
COOKING TIME: 10 MINUTES

For the salad
½ iceberg lettuce
Handful of fresh arugula leaves
6 sprigs of dill, chopped
2 mackerel
1 ½ cups sunflower oil
1 Tbsp olive oil for frying
1 tsp pine nuts
1 large tomato, peeled, seeded, and sliced
1 Tbsp currants, soaked

For the dressing
½ cup olive oil
Juice of ½ lemon
½ tsp mustard
1 tsp white wine vinegar
1 Tbsp chicken stock
Pinch of salt and freshly ground black pepper

1   Start by preparing the salad. Rinse the lettuce and arugula and shred. Rinse the dill and remove the stalks.

2   Gut the mackerel, remove the gills, and rinse thoroughly. Pat dry. Fry the mackerel in the sunflower oil and allow to cool before flaking.

3   Heat the olive oil in a pan and fry the pine nuts until golden brown.

4   Arrange the lettuce and arugula in a dome in the center of a serving bowl. Place the slices of fish and tomato around the center. Sprinkle the pine nuts, currants, and chopped dill over the fish.

5   Prepare the dressing by mixing together the olive oil, lemon juice, mustard, vinegar, stock, salt, and pepper, then drizzle over the salad.

Lentil bulgur

Moudardara

SERVES 5
COOKING TIME: 1 HOUR

12½ oz lentils
4¼ cups water
5½ oz bulgur (cracked wheat)
Pinch of salt and white pepper
⅓ cup olive oil
3 onions, peeled and sliced

1 Rinse the lentils and place them in a saucepan with the water. Bring to a boil, then reduce heat. Cover and simmer for 30 minutes until the lentils are almost tender.

2 Rinse the bulgur and add it to the saucepan. Season with salt. Simmer over low heat for about 15 minutes.

3 In the meantime, heat the olive oil in a pan and fry the onions over moderate heat until golden brown. Reserve one third of the quantity for garnishing. Add the remaining onions with their oil to the lentils saucepan. Season with white pepper and simmer for 10 minutes until the liquid is absorbed and the bulgur and lentils are tender. Pour in a serving dish and garnish with the reserved browned onions.

Hot mezze

Sultan's delight

Hunkar begendi

SERVES 6
COOKING TIME: 1 HOUR 30 MINUTES

3 Tbsp butter
2 medium onions, peeled and finely chopped
2 lb 3 oz leg of lamb, cubed
2 garlic cloves, peeled and crushed
2 large tomatoes, peeled, seeded, and diced
1 small sweet green pepper, seeded, and
   finely chopped
1¼ cups hot water
1 tsp salt
1 tsp peppercorns

For the eggplant purée
3 lb 5 oz eggplants
4½ oz butter
3 Tbsp all-purpose flour
1¾ cups warm milk
Pinch of salt
4 Tbsp grated mature kasar or cheddar cheese
Pinch of grated nutmeg

1 Heat the butter in a pan and fry the onions until softened, then add the lamb and cook over medium heat, stirring occasionally, for 10 minutes. Add the garlic, tomatoes, and pepper, and cook until the juice has evaporated.

2 Stir in the hot water, salt, and peppercorns, cover and bring to a boil. Lower heat and cook over medium heat for approximately 1 hour.

3 To prepare the eggplant purée, rinse the eggplants and pierce the skin in several places with toothpicks and cook over an open gas flame or charcoal fire, turning occasionally until the skin is charred and the flesh is tender.

4 In the meantime, melt the butter in a large saucepan, sprinkle over the flour and stir, then remove from heat.

5 Holding the eggplants by their stalks, scrape away the skin, then remove the stalks and add to the saucepan Mash the eggplants and place the saucepan over medium heat, blending together, and gradually adding in the warm milk and salt.

6 When the mixture bubbles, remove from heat, add the cheese and nutmeg, and stir well. Pour the eggplant purée into a serving bowl, hollow out the center and arrange the meat in its juices into the center. Serve hot.

Split pea croquettes
Fava keftedes

SERVES 4–6
COOKING TIME: 1 HOUR

1 lb 2 oz yellow split peas
1 onion, peeled and grated
Small bunch of parsley, finely chopped
6 oz breadcrumbs
6 oz feta cheese, crumbled
2 medium eggs, beaten
Pinch of salt and freshly ground black pepper
All-purpose flour, for coating the croquettes
Olive oil, for frying

1 Rinse the peas in a sieve under running water, then place in a large saucepan. Add water and bring to a boil.

2 Once boiled, add the onion and simmer over low heat for 50 minutes, until thick. Remove from heat and set aside to cool.

3 Add the parsley, breadcrumbs, cheese, eggs, salt, and pepper, and mix together to form a thick consistency.

4 Knead the mixture and shape into golf ball-sized balls. Coat each ball in flour and fry in olive oil until golden.

 LEBANON

Fried eggs with minced meat
Bayd bi kawarma

SERVES 4
COOKING TIME: 5 MINUTES

⅓ cup olive oil
7 oz lean lamb, minced
6 medium eggs
Pinch white pepper

1 Heat the olive oil in a pan and fry the minced meat until brown and tender.

2 Break the eggs over the meat and season with white pepper. Mix well and cook until the egg whites run dry. Transfer to a serving dish and serve immediately.

Fava beans and artichokes

Koukia me aginares

SERVES 4–6
COOKING TIME: 45 MINUTES

8 artichoke hearts, halved
2 Tbsp lemon juice
2 lb 3 oz fresh fava beans
½ cup olive oil
Small bunch of dill, finely chopped
2 fresh garlic leaves, chopped
Pinch of salt and freshly ground black pepper
2 Tbsp all-purpose flour
2 Tbsp white wine vinegar

1 Rub the artichoke hearts with the lemon juice and set aside. Top and tail the fava beans.

2 Heat the oil in a saucepan and sauté the dill and garlic leaves for a couple of minutes.

3 Add the beans and cover with 1 cup water. Simmer for 15 minutes. Add the artichokes, salt, and pepper. Stir well and simmer for about 20 minutes, or until the artichokes are almost tender.

4 In a bowl, dilute the flour in ⅓ cup water, then add the vinegar. Remove 3 to 4 tablespoons of liquid from the pan and stir into the flour mixture. Pour this mixture back into the pan, stir well, and cook for 5 minutes. Serve hot.

Rabbit in wine and garlic sauce

Kouneli me aspri saltsa

SERVES 4
COOKING TIME: 1 HOUR

Small rabbit, skinned, gutted, and cut into
    small portions
¾ cup white wine
½ cup olive oil
5 garlic cloves, peeled and crushed
Pinch of salt and freshly ground black pepper
2 oz all-purpose flour
2 sprigs of rosemary, chopped
Juice of 1 lemon

1 Place the rabbit pieces in a bowl with half the wine and marinate for 30 minutes.

2 Place the rabbit pieces in a pan with the oil, garlic, salt, and pepper, and lightly brown. Add the flour, rosemary, lemon juice, and remaining wine, and simmer for approximately 30 minutes or until the meat is tender and cooked.

Spinach pies

Spanakopita

SERVES 6
COOKING TIME: 40 MINUTES

½ cup olive oil
1 onion, peeled and finely chopped
3 scallions, finely chopped
2 garlic cloves, peeled and minced
2 lb 3 oz spinach leaves, rinsed
  and finely chopped
Small bunch of parsley, finely chopped
Small bunch of mint, finely chopped
2 medium eggs, lightly beaten
4 oz feta cheese, crumbled
3½ oz ricotta cheese
8 sheets filo pastry
2 Tbsp butter, for greasing

1 Preheat the oven to 375º F (190º C) and grease a 10 in square baking pan with butter.

2 Heat the olive oil in a pan and fry the onion, scallions, and garlic until lightly browned. Add in the spinach, parsley, and mint, and sauté briefly until the spinach is wilted. Remove from heat and set aside to cool.

3 In a bowl, mix together the eggs, feta, and ricotta cheeses, then stir into the spinach mixture and combine thoroughly.

4 Lay a sheet of filo pastry in the baking pan and lightly brush with olive oil. Then layer three more sheets of filo overlapping the first, each brushed with oil.

5 Spread the spinach and cheese mixture over the pastry and fold the overhanging pastry over the filling and brush with oil.

6 Layer the remaining four sheets of filo, each brushed with oil, over the mixture. Tuck the pastry around to seal the filling. Bake for 30 minutes or until golden. Once cooked, cut into squares, and serve hot.

Fried fish with tahini sauce

Samak makli ma el tarator

SERVES 4
COOKING TIME: 20 MINUTES

4 lb 6 oz red mullet
All-purpose flour, for coating the fish
4 cups vegetable oil
6 pita pockets
2 lemons, cut into wedges, to garnish

For the stuffing

1 Tbsp butter
Bunch of cilantro, finely chopped
1 garlic clove, peeled and crushed
Pinch of salt and white pepper

For the sauce

2 oz tahini
¼ cup lemon juice
¼ cup water
1 garlic clove, peeled and crushed
Salt and freshly ground black pepper

1 Clean and scale the fish. Rinse thoroughly and drain.

2 Prepare the stuffing by combining all the ingredients together and stuffing the fish with the mixture. Seal the fish at the sides with toothpicks.

3 Coat the fish with flour. Heat the vegetable oil in a frying pan and fry the fish over high heat for 5 to 7 minutes on each side, until tender and golden brown.

4 In the meantime, combine all the sauce ingredients together and mix well until smooth.

5 Carefully lift the fish out of the pan and drain on paper towels. Fry the pita bread in the same oil until golden brown. Arrange the fish on a serving dish and garnish with lemon wedges. Serve hot along with the fried bread and tahini sauce.

Eggplants with yogurt sauce

Fattet el batinjan

SERVES 4
COOKING TIME: 50 MINUTES

14 oz lean lamb, from the leg
3½ oz leeks, cut into chunks
1 oz fresh dill, chopped
2 bay leaves
2 cloves
2 lb 3 oz eggplants, cubed and soaked
   for 6 hours in salted water
2 oz all-purpose flour
¾ cup vegetable oil, for frying
Pinch of salt and white pepper
4 garlic cloves, peeled and crushed
3½ cups plain yoghurt
4 pita pockets, cut into pieces
2 oz pine nuts
Pinch of dried mint

1 Trim away any excess fat from the meat and cut into 1 in cubes. Transfer to a large saucepan and cover with water. Bring to a boil until the fat floats to the surface, then remove it with a large spoon. Add in the leeks, dill, bay leaves, and cloves. Cook the meat for about 20 minutes, or until tender.

2 In the meantime, rinse the eggplant cubes, drain, and toss in the flour. Heat half the vegetable oil in a pan and fry the eggplant cubes until brown. Drain on paper towels, then add to the meat. Season the mixture with salt and pepper and bring to a boil, then reduce heat and simmer for 10 minutes.

3 In a small saucepan mix the garlic with the yogurt and season with salt. Bring to a boil, stirring constantly, then remove from the heat and set aside.

4 Fry the bread in the remaining vegetable oil until golden brown, then drain on paper towels. Fry the pine nuts until brown, then drain and set aside.

5 Arrange the bread in a serving platter. Cover with the eggplant and meat cubes. Top with the yogurt and pine nuts and sprinkle with mint. Serve immediately.

Lamb kebab with eggplants

Patlicanli islim kebabi

SERVES 6
COOKING TIME: 1 HOUR 30 MINUTES

3 Tbsp butter
1 lb 10 oz cubed lamb
2 medium onions, peeled and finely chopped
2 garlic cloves, peeled and crushed
3 large tomatoes, peeled, seeded, and diced
2 mild green chilies, seeded, and finely chopped
4 cups hot water
1 tsp salt
6 long eggplants
Sunflower oil, to fry

To garnish
1 large green pepper, cut into squares
1 medium tomato, cut into squares
Pinch of thyme

1 Melt the butter in a saucepan, add the lamb, onions, and garlic, and cook over medium heat, stirring occasionally for 10 minutes.

2 Add the tomatoes and chilies, and cook for another 5 minutes until the meat is tender. Stir in the hot water and salt, cover, and cook over medium heat for approximately 1 hour, until the meat is tender.

3 Rinse and partially peel the eggplants in alternate lengthwise strips. Remove and discard the stalks and cut each eggplant into six ¾ in thick lengthwise strips. Place in a bowl and rub with salt to remove any bitter juices and leave for 25 minutes. Then rinse, dry, and fry the strips in sunflower oil until golden brown. Leave to drain on paper towels. Preheat the oven to 400º F (200º C).

4 Arrange six strips of eggplant diagonally in a small bowl so that each piece overhangs the bowl equally. Divide the meat into six equal quantities. Place one quantity of meat over the strips and fold over the overhanging eggplant strips to cover the meat. Carefully turn the bowl upside down onto an oven tray to form a dome. Repeat with the remaining ingredients. There should be six domes in total.

5 Garnish each dome with pepper and tomato squares placed on top of the dome and secured with a toothpick. Spoon over any remaining sauce and bake for 15 minutes. Sprinkle with thyme and serve hot.

Fried zucchini balls

Kolokythokeftedes

SERVES 4–6
COOKING TIME: 25 MINUTES

1 lb 2 oz potatoes
2 lb 3 oz onions, peeled
2 lb 3 oz zucchinis, grated
4 oz feta cheese, crumbled
1 tsp salt
Pinch of freshly ground black pepper
2 medium eggs, beaten
All-purpose flour, for coating the balls
Olive oil, for frying

1 Boil the potatoes and onions, then strain and chop into small pieces.

2 Combine the grated zucchinis, potatoes, onions, cheese, salt, pepper, and eggs, and mix together to form a thick consistency.

3 Knead the mixture and shape into golf ball-sized balls. Coat each ball in flour and fry in olive oil until golden. Drain on paper towels and serve hot.

 LEBANON

Fried potatoes with cilantro

Batata bil kouzbara

SERVES 5
COOKING TIME: 30 MINUTES

⅓ cup olive oil
2 lb 3 oz potatoes, peeled and cubed
2 garlic cloves, peeled
3½ oz fresh cilantro
2 Tbsp pine nuts
3 Tbsp coriander
1 Tbsp tomato paste
3 Tbsp lemon juice
Pinch of salt and freshly ground black pepper
½ tsp curry powder

1 Heat the olive oil in a pan and fry the potato cubes. Cook on medium heat until golden brown, then drain on paper towels.

2 Crush the garlic with the cilantro and fry with the pine nuts in the same pan for 3 minutes until golden brown. Stir in the potato cubes, coriander, tomato paste, and lemon juice. Season with salt, pepper, and the curry powder. Simmer over low heat for 3 minutes. Transfer to serving dish and serve immediately.

Stuffed mussels

Midye dolmasi

SERVES 10
COOKING TIME: 1 HOUR 35 MINUTES

40 medium mussels in shells
2 medium onions, peeled and finely chopped
½ tsp salt
½ tsp super fine sugar
⅓ cup olive oil
1¾ cups hot water
1 lemon, peeled and sliced

For the stuffing
4½ oz white rice
2 Tbsp currants
⅓ cup olive oil
⅓ cup sunflower oil
2 Tbsp pine nuts
6 medium onions, peeled and finely chopped
1 tsp cinnamon
1 tsp allspice
1 tsp white pepper
1 tsp salt
1 tsp sugar
⅓ cup hot water
½ bunch of fresh mint, chopped
Bunch of dill, chopped

1 Scrape the mussel shells with a knife or scrub with a brush. Soak in cold water while preparing the stuffing.

2 To make the stuffing, soak the rice in cold water for 30 minutes, then rinse thoroughly and drain. Soak the currants in warm water for about 15 minutes until they swell. Heat the olive and sunflower oils in a pan, add the pine nuts and onions, and brown slightly. Add the soaked rice and cook for 10 minutes. Then add the drained currants, spices, salt, sugar, and hot water, and cook over low heat for 15 minutes until the water has evaporated. Stir in the mint and dill, then set aside to cool.

3 Gently pry open each mussel with a knife without pulling the shells apart and remove the beard of the mussels, then rinse well and drain.

4 Place a tablespoon of rice stuffing into each shell and close tightly.

5 Add the onions into a large pan and place a sheet of damp waxed paper over them. Arrange the stuffed mussels on top in layers and add the salt, sugar, olive oil, and hot water.

6 Arrange the lemon slices over the mussels and place another sheet of damp waxed paper on top, weighted down with a plate. Cover and bring to a boil over high heat for approximately 40 minutes. When most of the liquid has evaporated and the mussels are opened, place in a serving dish with the onions and garnish with the lemon slices.

Chickpeas in yogurt sauce

Fattet el hommus bil laban

SERVES 4
COOKING TIME: 20 MINUTES

2 Tbsp butter
2 garlic cloves, peeled and crushed
1 tsp salt
1 Tbsp dried mint
1¾ cups plain yogurt
1 tsp paprika
¾ cup milk
4 pita pockets
1 lb 2 oz canned chickpeas, rinsed
3 Tbsp pine nuts
1 Tbsp dried mint
1 Tbsp paprika

1 Heat the butter in a pan and fry the garlic with the salt and dried mint until lightly browned. Remove from heat and transfer to a bowl. Strain the yogurt and mix with the garlic.

2 Preheat the oven to 375º F (190º C). Dissolve the paprika in the milk in a large bowl. Soak the bread in the milk for 30 seconds, then toast in the oven until brown. Break the toasted bread into pieces.

3 Arrange the bread in a shallow serving dish. Pour the yogurt over the bread and top with the chickpeas. Sprinkle with the pine nuts, dried mint, and paprika. Serve immediately.

 GREECE

Bean purée

Fava

SERVES 4
COOKING TIME: 1 HOUR

1 lb 2 oz dried fava beans
2 tsp salt
2 Tbsp olive oil
Juice of 1 lemon
1 scallion, finely chopped, to garnish

1 Soak the beans overnight in water. The following day, remove and discard the black tips and husks from the beans. Boil the beans in salted water for 30 minutes.

2 Strain the beans, place them in a saucepan, and cover with water. Boil for a further 30 minutes, stirring regularly. Add the olive oil and lemon juice, and stir well. Transfer to a serving bowl and garnish with the chopped scallions. Serve hot.

Cheese pies

Kallitsounia

SERVES 6
COOKING TIME: 40 MINUTES

For the dough
2 lb 3 oz all-purpose flour
2 cups water
1 tsp dried yeast
½ cup olive oil
Juice of 1 lemon
1 tsp salt

For the filling
2 medium eggs, lightly beaten
4 lb 6 oz feta cheese, crumbled
Small bunch of mint, finely chopped
½ tsp crushed coriander
Salt and freshly ground black pepper

For the coating
1 egg, lightly beaten
1 Tbsp sesame seeds

1 Prepare the dough by mixing all the ingredients together in a bowl, then cover with a towel and set aside to rise in a warm place for approximately 1 hour.

2 In the meantime, make the filling. In a bowl, mix together all the ingredients.

3 When the dough has risen, roll it out to a ¼ in thickness and cut into 4 in circles. You will need 24 circles in total. Preheat the oven to 400° F (200° C) and grease a baking pan. Place a spoonful of the filling into each of the dough circles and fold over to seal.

4 Glaze the top of the crescent-shaped parcels with egg and sprinkle with sesame seeds. Place on a baking tray and bake for 30 minutes or until golden brown.

Baked small fish

Bourtheto

SERVES 4–6
COOKING TIME: 25 MINUTES

1 lb 3 oz sardines or pilchards,
   rinsed and gutted
6 Tbsp olive oil
Pinch of salt and freshly ground black pepper
4 tomatoes, grated
1 onion, peeled and grated
Pinch of dried oregano
Small bunch of parsley, finely chopped

1 Preheat the oven to 375º F (190º C). Drizzle half the oil over the fish and place in an oiled baking pan. Season with salt and pepper.

2 In a bowl, mix the remaining oil with the tomatoes, onion, oregano, and parsley, and pour over the fish. Bake for 25 minutes. Serve hot.

Fava bean stew

Koukia

SERVES 4
COOKING TIME: 45 MINUTES

1 lb 2 oz dried fava beans
½ cup olive oil
2 onions, peeled and finely chopped
2 tomatoes, finely chopped
Small bunch of parsley, finely chopped
1 tsp cumin
4 bay leaves
Pinch of salt and freshly ground black pepper
2 cups water

1 Soak the beans in water overnight.

2 The following day remove and discard the eyes (the black tips of the beans) with a sharp knife and boil the beans in water for 30 minutes, then strain.

3 Heat the olive oil in a saucepan and brown the onions, then add in the tomatoes, parsley, cumin, bay leaves, salt, and pepper, and cook for 5 minutes.

4 Add the beans to the pan, along with the water, and simmer until the sauce thickens. Serve hot.

Moussaka

Mousakas

SERVES 6
COOKING TIME: 1 HOUR 45 MINUTES

4 Tbsp olive oil
2 lb 3 oz minced meat
2 onions, peeled and finely chopped
½ cup white wine
4 tomatoes, pulped
Salt and freshly ground black pepper
3 medium eggs, beaten
4 oz feta cheese, crumbled
4 oz breadcrumbs
2 lb 3 oz eggplants, cubed
2 lb 3 oz zucchinis, cubed
2 Tbsp butter, for greasing

For the béchamel sauce
4 Tbsp butter
8 Tbsp all-purpose flour
8½ cups milk
1 oz Parmesan cheese, grated
2 egg, yolks beaten
Pinch of salt, freshly ground black pepper,
   and nutmeg

1   Heat the olive oil in a pan and fry the minced meat and onions until lightly browned. Pour in the wine, add the tomatoes, season with salt and pepper, and cook for 30 minutes, stirring regularly. Then stir in the eggs, feta cheese, and breadcrumbs.

2   In a separate pan, fry the eggplants and zucchinis until lightly cooked.

3   Grease a 10 in square baking pan with the butter and alternate a layer of vegetables with a layer of meat. Repeat until the mixtures are finished. Preheat the oven to 375º F (190º C).

4   To make the sauce, melt the butter in a pan. Remove from heat and stir in the flour. Return to heat, gradually adding in the milk and stirring all the while, and simmer for 9 minutes until thick. Add the Parmesan and egg yolks. Stir until thick, then remove from heat and season.

5   Pour the sauce over the meat and vegetable mixture and bake for 1 hour until golden.

Octopus with wine and green olives

Htapodi krasato me prasines elies

SERVES 4–6
COOKING TIME: 35 MINUTES

½ cup olive oil
2 lb 3 oz octopus
½ cup red wine
Pinch of freshly ground black pepper
6½ oz green olives, sliced

1 Remove and discard the ink sacs from the octopus and rinse thoroughly. Chop into pieces. Heat the olive oil in a pan and gently fry the octopus for 20 minutes

2 Add the wine and pepper, and simmer for 15 minutes until soft. Add a little water if necessary. Sprinkle with olives and serve immediately.

Mashed potatoes

Batata mahrouseh bil zeit

SERVES 4
COOKING TIME: 25 MINUTES

1 lb 5 oz new or baking potatoes
⅓ cup olive oil
2 onions, peeled and chopped
2 Tbsp dried parsley
Pinch of salt and white pepper

To garnish
Olive oil
1 tomato, sliced
Fresh mint leaves

1 Rinse the potatoes and boil in salted water until cooked. Drain and peel, then mash to a purée in a large bowl.

2 Stir in the olive oil, onions, and parsley. Season with salt and pepper. Transfer the mashed potatoes to a serving dish. Drizzle with olive oil and garnish with the tomato slices and mint leaves.

Cabbage and rice pilaf

Lahanorizo

SERVES 4
COOKING TIME: 25 MINUTES

½ cup olive oil
1 onion, peeled and finely chopped
1 small cabbage, chopped
2 cups water
3 tomatoes, grated
15 oz uncooked rice
Pinch of salt and freshly ground black pepper

1 Heat the olive oil in a large saucepan and fry the onion. Add the cabbage, stir, then add the water.

2 Add the grated tomatoes to the pan, stir, and cook for 10 minutes. Finally, add the rice and, stirring occasionally, cook until the rice is cooked through and the water has been absorbed. Season with salt and pepper.

 GREECE

Stuffed zucchini flowers

Anthi

SERVES 6
COOKING TIME: 40 MINUTES

40 zucchini flowers

For the filling
3 tomatoes, grated
2 onions, peeled and finely chopped
½ cup olive oil
Small bunch of dill, finely chopped
Small bunch of parsley, finely chopped
Small bunch of mint, finely chopped
1lb 2 oz white rice
Pinch of salt and freshly ground black pepper

1 Pick the zucchini flowers fresh so they will be open. Rinse them, remove the stems, and set aside while preparing the stuffing.

2 In a bowl add the tomatoes, onions, olive oil, dill, parsley, mint, rice, salt, and pepper and mix together with ½ cup water.

3 Stuff the flowers with the mixture and place them in a pot. Cover with water and place a plate over them to stop the flowers from opening. Simmer until all the water has been absorbed. Serve hot.

Sis kebab with yogurt

Yogurtlu sis kebab

SERVES 4
COOKING TIME: 1 HOUR 30 MINUTES

For the marinade
4 medium onions, peeled and finely chopped
4 garlic cloves, peeled and crushed
¾ cup sunflower oil
1 tsp salt
Pinch of freshly ground black pepper

For the sauce
1 medium onion, peeled and finely chopped
1 garlic clove, peeled and crushed
2 Tbsp butter
2 mild green chilies, seeded, and finely chopped
4 large tomatoes, peeled, seeded, and diced
1 tsp salt

For the kebabs and sis kofte
2 lb 3 oz cubed lamb
1 green chili, seeded and finely chopped
½ red pepper, finely chopped
1 small onion, peeled and finely chopped
2 garlic cloves, peeled and crushed
7 sprigs of parsley, chopped
Pinch of chili flakes
½ tsp salt
Pinch of freshly ground black pepper
7 oz finely minced lamb

1 Tbsp butter
3 small pita bread
Pinch of salt
Pinch of sumac
1 tsp thyme
1 long eggplant
¾ cup plain yogurt

1 Start by preparing the marinade. In a large bowl, place the onions, garlic, oil, salt, and pepper. Add in the cubed lamb and marinate overnight.

2 The following day, prepare the sauce. Heat the butter in a pan and lightly brown the onion and garlic. Add the chilies and stir for a few minutes, then add the tomatoes and salt, and cook over moderate heat until soft.

3 Thread the marinated cubed lamb onto 8 skewers and set aside.

4 Prepare the sis kofte. In a large bowl, mix together the chili, pepper, onion, garlic, parsley, chili flakes, salt, and pepper, then mix in the minced lamb. With wet hands squeeze an egg-sized portion of the mixture around a broad metal skewer, flattening and lengthening out. Repeat until all the mixture has been used.

5 Grill the skewers of cubed lamb and kofte under medium heat until cooked, turning regularly to ensure all sides are evenly cooked.

6 Cut the pita bread into small squares and lightly fry in the butter. Arrange in the center of a large serving dish and sprinkle with the salt, sumac, and thyme. Spoon half of the tomato sauce over the pita. Rinse and peel the eggplant in alternate strips, slice into rounds, and fry until tender.

7 Beat the yogurt and spoon over the pita. Carefully remove the sis kofte from the skewers, cut in half, and arrange with the meat skewers around the pita. Arrange the eggplant rounds over the pita.

Chickpeas in cumin and olive oil

Balila

SERVES 4
COOKING TIME: 40 MINUTES

14 oz dried chickpeas, soaked overnight
   in ½ tsp baking soda

For the sauce
2 garlic cloves, peeled and crushed
⅓ cup olive oil
1 Tbsp cumin
Pinch of salt

1 Rinse the soaked chickpeas and place in a pan. Cover with water and bring to a boil. Reduce heat to medium and simmer for about 30 minutes, until cooked.

2 In the meantime, prepare the sauce. Mix the garlic with the olive oil, cumin, and salt in a serving bowl. Drain the chickpeas and add them to the bowl. Mix well and serve immediately.

 LEBANON

Chicken liver in pomegranate sauce

Kasbat el dajaj bi dibsil rouman

SERVES 5
COOKING TIME: 15 MINUTES

1 lb 2 oz chicken liver
⅓ cup olive oil
Pinch salt and freshly ground black pepper
¼ cup lemon juice
1 Tbsp pomegranate paste

1 Trim any excess fat from the chicken liver and cut into cubes. Heat the olive oil in a pan and fry the livers until browned and almost tender. Season with salt and pepper.

2 Add the lemon juice and pomegranate paste to the pan, mix well, and cook until the meat is tender. Transfer to a serving dish and serve immediately.

Stuffed kofte

Icli kofte

SERVES 8
COOKING TIME: 30 MINUTES

For the filling
2 Tbsp sunflower oil
2 lb 3 oz minced beef
3 lb 5 oz onions, peeled and finely chopped
1 tsp salt
1 tsp freshly ground black pepper
1 tsp red pepper
10½ oz ground walnuts
10½ oz blanched pistachio nuts

For the kofte
1 lb 2 oz lean minced beef
3 medium potatoes, peeled and grated
2 Tbsp semolina
1 small onion, peeled and finely chopped
1 tsp salt
½ tsp freshly ground black pepper
½ tsp red pepper
1¾ cup water
3 lb 5 oz fine bulgur

Sunflower oil, for frying

1 Start by preparing the filling. Heat the oil in a pan and fry the minced meat until the juices have evaporated. Add the onions and cook for 5 minutes, then add the salt, black and red pepper, and nuts. Mix well and remove from heat. Shape the mixture into finger shapes and set aside to cool.

2 To make the kofte, thoroughly knead together (or blend in a mixer) all the ingredients, excluding the water and bulgur, until a smooth dough is formed, then add the water and bulgur. Continue to knead the mixture in a bowl until it forms a paste.

3 Roll the kofte mixture into walnut-sized balls, hollow out the centers and stuff with the filling. You will need about 48 balls in total. Seal each hole by smoothing over with wet hands so there are no cracks. Place the balls under a damp cloth and when all are ready, fry them in sunflower oil for 8 to 10 minutes, or until golden brown. Drain on paper towels and serve hot.

Stuffed vegetables

Gemista

SERVES 5
COOKING TIME: 1 HOUR 20 MINUTES

Vegetables for stuffing
5 tomatoes
2 eggplants
2 zucchinis
2 red peppers
2 potatoes

For the filling
2 onions, peeled and finely chopped
½ cup olive oil
Small bunch of dill, finely chopped
Small bunch of parsley, finely chopped
1 lb 2 oz white rice
Pinch of salt and freshly ground black pepper
3 tomatoes, grated
4 oz feta cheese, crumbled

1 Preheat the oven to 375º F (190º C). Hollow out all the vegetables for stuffing, set them aside, and place their contents (except for the peppers) in a large bowl.

2 To make the filling, add the onions, half the olive oil, dill, parsley, rice, salt, and pepper to the bowl and mix together.

3 Salt the hollowed insides of the vegetables and stuff them with the mixture. Place them in a deep baking dish.

4 Pour the grated tomatoes and remaining oil over the vegetables. Bake in the oven for approximately 1 hour 10 minutes. Sprinkle the cheese over the vegetables and bake for another 5 minutes, or until the cheese melts. Serve hot.

Squid in lemon and cilantro sauce

Sabbidej bahri

SERVES 6
COOKING TIME: 30 MINUTES

2 lb 3 oz squid
6 garlic cloves, peeled
7 oz fresh cilantro
Pinch of salt and white pepper
3½ oz butter
¾ cup lemon juice
Rind of 1 lemon
¾ cup fish stock
Lemon wedges and cilantro, to garnish

1 Clean the squids and cut into squares. Boil in salted water for 10 minutes, then drain and set aside.

2 Blend the garlic, cilantro, and salt in a food processor until smooth. Heat the butter in a saucepan, then add the garlic mixture with the squid squares. Fry for 5 minutes, then mix in the lemon juice, lemon rind, and fish stock, and season with salt and pepper. Bring the mixture to a boil for 10 minutes.

3 Transfer the squids and sauce to a serving dish. Garnish with lemon wedges and cilantro. Serve immediately.

 LEBANON

Spicy potatoes

Batata harra

SERVES 4
COOKING TIME: 15 MINUTES

2 cups vegetable oil
2 lb 3 oz potatoes, peeled and cubed
1 Tbsp butter
3 oz coriander
1 tsp chili paste
Pinch of salt, freshly ground black pepper,
    and paprika
Fresh cilantro, to garnish

1 Heat the oil in a pan and fry the potato cubes until golden brown. Drain on paper towels.

2 Heat the butter in a separate pan and fry the coriander. Mix in the potatoes, chili paste, salt, pepper, and paprika. Transfer to a serving dish and garnish with cilantro. Serve immediately.

Fried kibbeh balls

Kebbeh maklieh

SERVES 4
COOKING TIME: 1 HOUR 15 MINUTES

For the stuffing

3 Tbsp vegetable oil
2 onions, peeled and finely chopped
7 oz lean lamb, coarsely minced
1 cinnamon stick
Pinch of salt and white pepper
1 tsp sumac

For the meat shells

1 lb 2 oz extra lean lamb from the leg, cubed
9 oz brown bulgur
Pinch of salt
½ tsp paprika
8 Tbsp iced water
Corn oil, for frying

1 Start by making the stuffing. Heat the oil in a pan and fry the onions until golden brown. Add the minced lamb and cinnamon stick. Cook until the juices have evaporated and the meat begins to brown. Season with salt and pepper. Remove from heat and set aside. Discard the cinnamon stick and mix in the sumac.

2 To prepare the meat shells, divide the lamb into batches and process to a paste-like consistency using a food processor, then transfer to a large bowl. Add in the bulgur, salt, and paprika. Knead to a paste with moistened hands.

3 Process the mixture again in four batches, adding two tablespoons of iced water to each batch, until the paste turns smooth. Combine in a bowl and knead again for about 1 minute, with moistened hands.

4 Divide the meat mixture into 20 egg-size portions and roll into balls. Make a hole in each ball with your finger, then work around the hole, pressing gently until you have a thin, round shell. Fill each shell with one tablespoon of the stuffing, then gently close up the hole, again with moistened hands, and place on a tray. Larger quantities of kibbeh may be prepared in advance and frozen for later use.

5 Heat the corn oil in a pan and deep-fry the kibbeh balls in batches until completely browned. Lift out with a slotted spoon and drain on paper towels. Serve immediately.

Chicken wings with cilantro

Jawaneh el dajaj bil kouzbara

SERVES 4
COOKING TIME: 15 MINUTES

24 chicken wings
1¾ cups vegetable oil
4 garlic cloves, peeled and crushed
Bunch of cilantro, finely chopped
1 Tbsp pomegranate paste
⅓ cup lemon juice
Pinch of salt and freshly ground black pepper

For the garnish
Lettuce leaves
Fresh cilantro leaves
Lemon wedges

1 Rinse the chicken wings in cold water and drain. Heat the oil in a pan and fry the wings in batches until golden brown and almost tender.

2 Mix in the garlic, cilantro, pomegranate paste, and lemon juice. Season with salt and pepper.

3 Transfer the chicken wings to a serving dish and drizzle with the cooking juice. Garnish with lettuce leaves, cilantro, and lemon wedges.

Onion pie

Kremidopita

SERVES 6
COOKING TIME: 40 MINUTES

½ cup olive oil
2 lb 3 oz onions, peeled and finely chopped
1 lb 2 oz feta cheese, crumbled
4 medium eggs, lightly beaten
Small bunch of dill, finely chopped
Salt and freshly ground black pepper
8 sheets filo pastry
Olive oil, for brushing the pastry

1 Preheat the oven to 375º F (190º C). Grease a 10 in square baking pan.

2 Heat the olive oil in a pan and fry the onions until lightly browned. Remove from heat and add the feta, eggs, dill, salt, and pepper and mix together.

3 Lay a sheet of filo pastry in the baking pan and lightly brush with olive oil. Then layer three more sheets of filo pastry overlapping and overhanging the first, each brushed with oil.

4 Spread the onion and cheese mixture over the pastry and fold the overhanging pastry over the filling, then brush with oil.

5 Layer the remaining four sheets of filo, each brushed with oil, over the mixture. Tuck the pastry around to seal the filling. Bake for 40 minutes or until golden. Once cooked, cut into squares and serve hot.

Cretan cookie

Sarikopites

SERVES 4–6
COOKING TIME: 10 MINUTES

For the dough
1 lb 2 oz all-purpose flour
¾ cup water
3 Tbsp olive oil
2 Tbsp lemon juice or raki
1 tsp salt

For the filling
1 lb 2 oz ricotta cheese

For the syrup
½ cup light honey
3½ oz super fine sugar
½ cup water

1 To prepare the dough, knead together the flour, water, half the olive oil, lemon juice or raki, and salt.

2 Roll out the dough and cut into 4 x 8 in strips. You will need 20 strips in total.

3 Spread the ricotta cheese along the strips and twist each strip into a spiral, sealing at each end by folding over and smoothing water over the ends. Fry the strips in the remaining olive oil until golden brown, then drain and place in a serving dish.

4 To make the syrup, boil the honey, sugar, and water for 5 minutes. Pour the hot syrup over the strips and serve hot.

Poached eggs with yogurt

Cilbir

SERVES 2
COOKING TIME: 5–8 MINUTES

2 garlic cloves, peeled and crushed
4 Tbsp plain yogurt
4 cups water
Pinch of salt
1 Tbsp white wine vinegar
4 medium eggs
1 Tbsp butter
Pinch of paprika
Bread, to serve

1 In a bowl, blend together the crushed garlic and yogurt.

2 In a large shallow saucepan bring the water, salt, and vinegar to a boil, then lower heat. Break one egg at a time into a bowl and slide carefully into the hot water making sure the eggs do not stick together. Cover and cook for 2 minutes.

3 When the whites have set and the yolks are veiled, carefully remove the poached eggs with a slotted spoon and place on a serving dish. Pour the yogurt over the eggs.

4 Melt the butter in a small pan, stir in the paprika, and pour over the yogurt-topped eggs. Serve hot with bread.

Stuffed dumplings with yogurt

Manti

SERVES 4
COOKING TIME: 30 MINUTES

For the pastry
10½ oz all-purpose flour
1 tsp salt
3 Tbsp olive oil
1 medium egg, beaten
4 Tbsp water

For the filling
7 oz minced lamb
1 medium onion, peeled and grated
½ tsp salt
Pinch of freshly ground black pepper

For the tomato sauce
3½ oz butter
3 medium tomatoes, peeled, seeded, and diced
Pinch of salt
1 tsp chili flakes
1 tsp dried mint

For the yogurt sauce
3 garlic cloves, peeled and crushed
1¾ cups plain yogurt

1 Start by making the pastry. Sieve the flour into a bowl, hollow out the center and add the salt, olive oil, egg, and water and mix together. Knead to a paste, cover with a damp cloth, and set aside for 30 minutes. Then divide into two equal portions and place one under a damp cloth.

2 Flour a board, roll out one of the pieces to a ¼ in thickness, then cut into long 1 in wide strips, then cut into squares. Repeat with the other portion of pastry. There should be 80 squares in total.

3 To prepare the filling, mix together the lamb, onion, salt, and pepper in a bowl. Place 1 teaspoon of the filling onto each square of pastry, gather the corners, and fold into the opposite corners to form little parcels, sealing the corners with water.

4 Bring a pan of salted water to a boil and gently drop the dumplings in, one at a time, stirring occasionally to prevent them sticking together. Simmer for 15 minutes or until the parcels rise to the surface, then cook for another 2 minutes. Remove from heat with a slotted spoon, place in soup bowls and keep warm.

5 To prepare the tomato sauce, melt the butter in a frying pan, add the tomatoes and salt, and cook over medium heat until softened. Just before removing from the heat, add the chili flakes and mint, stir well, and transfer to a bowl.

6 Prepare the yogurt sauce. In a small bowl, stir the garlic into the yogurt. To serve, spoon the tomato and yogurt sauces over the dumplings and serve hot.

TURKEY

Sardines in grape leaves

Asma yapraginda sardalya

SERVES 10
COOKING TIME: 15 MINUTES

50 sardines
50 grape leaves

For the marinade
2 tsp salt
Juice of 2 lemons
1 tsp white pepper
2½ cups olive oil

1   Keeping heads and tails intact, gut and remove the backbone of the sardines. Scrape off the scales, rinse well, and drain, then place in a bowl.

2   Prepare marinade by mixing together the salt, lemon juice, pepper, and olive oil, then pour over the sardines and set aside for 15 minutes.

3   In the meantime, scald the fresh grape leaves in boiling water, then dip in cold water to preserve their color. If the leaves are preserved in brine, soak in warm water, then rinse thoroughly to remove excess salt before scalding.

4   Place each leaf on a clean surface, glossy-side down and veins facing upwards. Lay a sardine across the base of each leaf and roll up so that the head and tail stick out at either end. Brush each leaf with olive oil from the marinade.

5   Grill each leaf, starting with the flap side first, then turn over. Grill for approximately 7 to 10 minutes or until the leaves turn a yellowish-green color. Place on a serving dish and serve hot.

 LEBANON

Lebanese sausage in lemon sauce

Makanek

SERVES 4
COOKING TIME: 15 MINUTES

2 Tbsp vegetable oil
1 lb 12 oz lamb or beef sausages
Juice of 1 large lemon

Heat the oil in a pan and fry the sausages on all sides for about 12 minutes. Pour in the lemon juice and cook for another 3 minutes until tender. Transfer the sausages to a serving dish. Drizzle with the lemon cooking sauce and serve immediately.

Salads

Country salad
Choriatiki

SERVES 4

2 firm tomatoes, sliced
2 small cucumbers, sliced
1 green pepper, sliced
1 small onion, peeled and finely chopped
3½ oz feta cheese, cubed
4 Tbsp olive oil
Pinch of salt
1 Tbsp white wine vinegar
1 tsp dried oregano
6 black olives

1 Place the tomatoes, cucumbers, pepper, onion, and feta in a bowl and mix together.

2 In a separate bowl mix together the olive oil, salt, vinegar, and oregano. Pour this mixture over the vegetables and garnish with the olives.

 LEBANON

Cabbage salad
Salatat el malfouf

SERVES 4
COOKING TIME: 15 MINUTES

For the salad
1 lb 2 oz cabbage, chopped
4 sprigs of fresh mint, shredded
1 Tbsp dried mint
2 tomatoes, sliced

For the dressing
⅓ cup lemon juice
¾ cup olive oil
Pinch of salt and white pepper

1 Prepare the salad by mixing the cabbage with the fresh and dried mint and tomatoes in a large serving bowl.

2 To make the dressing, mix the lemon juice with olive oil and season with salt and white pepper.

3 Place the salad in a large serving bowl, drizzle the dressing over it, and toss well before serving.

Bean salad

Fasulye piyazi

SERVES 6

1 lb 2 oz green string beans, soaked overnight
3 large tomatoes
2 medium onions, peeled and finely sliced
2 eggs, hard-boiled, chopped
6 black olives and a sprig of parsley, to garnish

For the dressing
½ cup olive oil
Juice of ½ lemon
Bunch of parsley, chopped
1 Tbsp white wine vinegar
Pinch of salt
½ tsp paprika

1 Rinse and drain the soaked string beans. Place in a pan, cover with water, and bring to a boil. Simmer until the beans are tender, drain, and cool, then place in a serving bowl.

2 Peel, seed, and dice the tomatoes and add to the bowl, along with the onions and mix together.

3 Prepare the dressing by mixing together the olive oil, lemon juice, parsley, vinegar, salt, and paprika, then pour over the salad. Garnish with the eggs, olives, and parsley.

Thyme salad

Salatat el za'atar

SERVES 4
COOKING TIME: 10 MINUTES

14 oz fresh thyme
2 small onions, peeled and sliced
14 oz tomatoes, cut into wedges

For the dressing
1 garlic clove, peeled and crushed
¼ cup lemon juice
⅓ cup olive oil
Pinch of salt and white pepper

1 Rinse the thyme, pat dry, and transfer to a large bowl.

2 Prepare the dressing by mixing the garlic with the lemon juice and olive oil. Season with salt and pepper. Drizzle the dressing over the thyme and toss well.

3 Transfer the thyme to a serving dish. Top with the onions and garnish with the tomato wedges.

Beet and cabbage salad

Salatat el chamandar wal malfouf

SERVES 4
COOKING TIME: 45 MINUTES

14 oz beets
1 lb 2 oz cabbage, finely chopped

For the dressing
2 garlic cloves, peeled and crushed
¼ cup lemon juice
⅓ cup olive oil
Pinch of salt and white pepper

1 Rinse the beets well, place them in a pressure cooker, and steam for 30 to 45 minutes, until tender. Drain and rinse in cold water. Peel the beets and cut one into half circles and reserve for garnishing. Cut the remaining beets into medium-size cubes.

2 Prepare the dressing by mixing the garlic with the lemon juice and olive oil. Season with salt and white pepper.

3 Drizzle the dressing over the cabbage in a large bowl and toss well. Transfer the salad to a serving dish, then top the center with beet cubes and garnish with the reserved half circles.

LEBANON

Lebanese salad

Salatat Loubnanieh

SERVES 4

For the salad
4 cucumbers, sliced
2 tomatoes, cubed
6 scallions, coarsely chopped
Small bunch of fresh watercress
Small bunch of fresh parsley
Small bunch of fresh mint
1 green pepper, cubed
1 lettuce heart, shredded

For the dressing
2 garlic cloves, peeled and crushed
¼ cup lemon juice
½ cup olive oil
Pinch of salt and white pepper

1 Prepare the salad by rinsing all the vegetables and green leaves. Drain well and transfer to a large bowl.

2 Make the dressing by mixing the garlic with the lemon juice and olive oil. Season with salt and white pepper. Drizzle the dressing over the salad and toss well.

Greek salad

Horiatiki

SERVES 4

3 Tbsp olive oil
1 Tbsp lemon juice
1 tsp dried oregano
Pinch of salt and freshly ground black pepper
4 tomatoes, sliced
1 onion, peeled and thinly sliced
1 cucumber, diced
4½ oz feta cheese, cubed
16 kalamata olives

1 In a small bowl, mix together the olive oil, lemon juice, oregano, salt, and pepper, and set aside.

2 In a separate bowl, mix together the tomatoes, onion, cucumber, feta, and olives. Transfer to a serving bowl and pour the olive oil mixture over the salad and toss well.

 LEBANON

Parsley salad

Tabouleh

SERVES 4
COOKING TIME: 15 MINUTES

For the tabouleh
14 oz parsley, finely chopped
3½ oz fresh mint, finely chopped
1 small onion, peeled and finely chopped
1 tsp salt
Pinch of freshly ground black pepper
2 oz fine bulgur
2 large tomatoes, seeded and finely chopped
Cabbage leaves, to garnish

For the dressing
⅓ cup lemon juice
⅓ cup olive oil
1 Tbsp lemon rind
Pinch of salt and white pepper

1 Rinse the parsley and mint and drain. In a small bowl, rub the chopped onion with the salt and black pepper and set aside.

2 Rinse the bulgur and drain in a fine strainer, then transfer to a large bowl. Add the parsley, mint, tomatoes, and onion to the bowl.

3 Prepare the dressing by mixing the lemon juice with the olive oil and lemon rind. Season with salt and white pepper. Drizzle the dressing over the salad and mix well. Transfer the tabouleh to a serving dish and garnish with cabbage leaves.

Shepherd's salad

Coban salatasi

SERVES 6

3 large tomatoes, peeled, seeded, and chopped
3 mild green chilies
4 scallions
4 sprigs of parsley
2 small cucumbers
8 black olives and 4 small chopped radishes,
　to garnish

For the dressing
½ cup olive oil
Juice of 1 lemon
1 Tbsp white wine vinegar
Pinch of salt and freshly ground black pepper

1 Place the tomatoes in a salad bowl. Finely chop the chilies, scallions, and parsley, and add to the bowl.

2 Peel and chop the cucumbers and mix in with the other ingredients in the bowl.

3 Prepare the dressing by mixing together the olive oil, lemon juice, vinegar, and salt and pepper, then pour over the salad. Garnish with the olives and the radishes.

 GREECE

Beet salad

Patzarosalata

SERVES 4
COOKING TIME: 35 MINUTES

2 lb 3 oz beets
½ cup olive oil
3 Tbsp white wine vinegar
10½ oz strained yogurt
4 garlic cloves, peeled and crushed
3 oz roughly ground walnuts
Pinch of salt

1 Boil, peel, then dice the beets. Place them in a serving bowl.

2 In a separate bowl, blend the olive oil together with the vinegar, yogurt, garlic and walnuts. Pour this mixture over the beets. Add a pinch of salt, stir, and chill before serving.

TURKEY

Bulgur salad
Kisir

SERVES 10
COOKING TIME: 30 MINUTES

12½ oz fine bulgur
1 cup hot water
1 Tbsp red pepper purée
2 Tbsp tomato purée
½ cup olive oil
Juice of 1 lemon
1 tsp salt
½ tsp chili flakes
2 large tomatoes
½ bunch parsley, chopped
½ bunch fresh mint, chopped
½ bunch scallions, chopped
8–10 lettuce leaves, to garnish

1 Place the bulgur in a large mixing bowl. Pour over the hot water, stir, cover, and let stand for 30 minutes.

2 Add the pepper and tomato purées, olive oil, lemon juice, salt, and chili flakes to the bulgur and knead together.

3 Peel, seed, and dice the tomatoes. Add to the bulgur along with the parsley, mint, and scallions.

4 Place the bulgur and the above ingredients in a serving bowl and mix together. Garnish with lettuce leaves around the edges.

 TURKEY

Eggplant salad
Patlican salatasi

SERVES 10
COOKING TIME: 30 MINUTES

8 medium eggplants
Juice of 2 lemons
2 cups olive oil
1 tsp salt
Sprig of parsley and a few black olives, to garnish
Pita bread, to serve

1 Pierce the skin of the eggplants in several places with a toothpick or skewer and cook over an open flame until the skin has charred and the flesh is soft. Scrape off the charred skin, cut away the stalks, then cut the eggplants in half lengthwise and scrape out the seeds. Place the eggplants in a bowl.

2 Add the lemon juice, olive oil, and salt to the bowl, then mash together to form a smooth purée. Transfer to a serving dish and garnish with a sprig of parsley and black olives. Serve with hot pita bread.

Potato and egg salad

Patatosalata me avga

SERVES 6
COOKING TIME: 30 MINUTES

3 medium potatoes
6 eggs
2 tomatoes, sliced
1 onion, peeled and sliced
2 Tbsp finely chopped parsley
Small cucumber, sliced
1 Tbsp dried oregano
3 oz black olives
½ cup olive oil
2 Tbsp white wine vinegar
½ tsp salt
Pinch of freshly ground black pepper

1 Boil the potatoes until tender, then peel them. Hardboil the eggs, then remove the shell.

2 Cut the potatoes and eggs into slices and place in a salad bowl. Add the tomatoes, onion, parsley, cucumber, oregano, and olives to the bowl and refrigerate for approximately 20 minutes, or until cold.

3 Place the olive oil, vinegar, salt, and pepper in a small bowl and mix together, then drizzle over the salad.

 LEBANON

Tomato, onion, and garlic salad

Salatat el banadoora bil basal wal toum

SERVES 4

4 large tomatoes, cubed
1 onion, peeled and finely sliced
Small bunch of parsley, chopped
Fresh mint leaves, to garnish

For the dressing
1 garlic clove, peeled and crushed
¼ cup lemon juice
⅓ cup olive oil
Pinch of salt

1 In a large bowl, mix the tomatoes with the onion.

2 To prepare the dressing, mix the garlic with lemon juice and olive oil. Season with salt. Drizzle the dressing over the tomatoes and onion and toss well. Transfer to a serving dish and garnish with the parsley and mint leaves.

Pastries

Fresh oregano pastries

Fatayer bil za'atar

SERVES 5
COOKING TIME: 30 MINUTES

For the dough
1 lb 5 oz all-purpose flour
¼ oz dry yeast
1¾ cup warm water
Pinch of salt

For the filling
3½ oz fresh oregano
2 Tbsp toasted sesame seeds
½ tsp sumac
½ cup olive oil

1 Start by preparing the dough. In a large bowl, sieve the flour and hollow the center. Dissolve the yeast in the warm water and add to the bowl along with the salt. Knead well until the dough is soft and springy. Cover with a damp cloth and set aside for at least 30 minutes until the dough has doubled in size.

2 To make the filling, mix the fresh oregano with the sesame seeds, sumac, and olive oil.

3 Preheat the oven to 400° F (200° C). Roll out the dough on a lightly floured surface to a ¼ in thickness, then cut into 4 in circles. There should be 40 circles in total.

4 Place one level tablespoon of filling on the lower half of each circle. Bring the top half over to cover the filling and pinch the edges firmly to seal. Arrange the pastries on a lightly greased baking tray and bake for 15 minutes.

Meat triangles

Sambousek bil lahm

SERVES 4
COOKING TIME: 30 MINUTES

For the dough
14 oz all-purpose flour
3 oz butter
Pinch of salt
⅔ cup water

For the filling
2 Tbsp butter
3 onions, peeled and chopped
14 oz minced lamb
2 Tbsp pine nuts
Pinch of salt, freshly ground black and white pepper

Vegetable oil, for deep frying

1 Start by making the dough. In a large bowl, sieve the flour and hollow the center. Add in the butter and salt and knead well. Add the water gradually and knead for 5 to 6 minutes until the dough is soft and springy. Cover the bowl with a damp cloth and leave to rest for at least 30 minutes.

2 In the meantime prepare the filling. Heat the butter in a pan and fry the onions until almost tender. Mix in the lamb and pine nuts, and cook until tender and golden brown. Season with salt and black and white pepper, and set aside to cool.

3 Roll out the dough on a lightly floured surface to a ¼ in thickness, then cut into 4 in circles. There should be 50 circles in total.

4 Place one level tablespoon of filling in the center of each circle and bring up the edges together at three points to form a triangle. Pinch the edges together to seal the pastries. Fry the meat triangles in hot vegetable oil for 20 minutes until golden brown.

Meat pies

Lahm bil ajeen

SERVES 5
COOKING TIME: 30 MINUTES

For the dough

14 oz all-purpose flour
3 oz butter
Pinch of salt
¼ oz dry yeast
¾ cup warm water

For the filling

3 oz ghee
2 onions, peeled and chopped
3 oz pine nuts
12½ oz minced lamb
Pinch of salt
½ tsp freshly ground black pepper
½ tsp cinnamon
⅓ cup plain yogurt
1 Tbsp pomegranate paste
1 tomato, cubed

1 Start by preparing the dough. In a large bowl, sieve the flour and hollow the center. Add in the butter and salt and knead well. Dissolve the yeast in the warm water and add to the bowl. Knead the mixture until the dough is soft and springy. Cover with a damp cloth and set aside for at least 30 minutes until the dough has doubled in size.

2 In the meantime, prepare the filling. Heat the ghee in a pan and fry the onions with the pine nuts until golden brown. Add in the minced lamb and cook until brown. Season with salt, pepper, and cinnamon, then remove from heat and leave to cool. Mix in the yogurt, pomegranate paste, and tomato cubes.

3 Preheat the oven to 400° F (200° C). Roll out the dough on a lightly floured surface to a ¼ in thickness. Cut into 4 in circles. You will need 20 circles in total.

4 Place one level tablespoon of filling in the center of each circle, spreading it slightly with the back of a spoon. Arrange on a lightly greased baking tray. Bake for 10 minutes until crispy.

Small meat pasties

Kimathopitakia

SERVES 8–10
COOKING TIME: 15 MINUTES

For the dough
2 lb 3 oz all-purpose flour
2 eggs, beaten
¾ cup milk
1 tsp baking powder
Pinch of salt

For the filling
4 Tbsp olive oil
2 lb 3 oz lean minced meat
3 onions, peeled and finely chopped
Pinch of salt, pepper, and cinnamon
Small bunch of parsley, chopped
Small bunch of fresh mint, chopped

¾ cup olive oil, for frying

1 Make the dough by mixing together the flour, eggs, milk, baking powder, and salt. Knead well until a soft, springy dough is formed. Roll out the dough on a floured surface and cut into 4 in circles. You will need 50 circles in total.

2 Prepare the filling by heating the oil in a pan and browning the meat with the onions. Season with the salt, pepper, and cinnamon. Add the parsley and mint and stir well.

3 Place a tablespoon of filling in the center of each dough circle. Pull the dough over to form crescent shaped pasties. Fry the pasties in the oil until golden brown.

Meat and pine nut pizza

Sfiha bil lahm

SERVES 5
COOKING TIME: 30 MINUTES

For the dough
14 oz all-purpose flour
3 oz butter
Pinch of salt
¼ oz dry yeast
¾ cup warm water

For the filling
2 Tbsp butter
2 onions, peeled and chopped
2 Tbsp pine nuts
1 lb 2 oz minced lamb
Pinch of salt and freshly ground black pepper
¼ tsp ground cinnamon
2 tomatoes, cubed

1 Start by preparing the dough. In a large bowl, sieve the flour and hollow the center. Add in the butter and salt and knead well. Dissolve the yeast in the warm water and add to the bowl. Knead the mixture until the dough is soft and springy. Cover with a damp cloth and set aside for at least 30 minutes until the dough has doubled in size.

2 In the meantime, prepare the filling. Melt the butter in a pan and fry the onions with the pine nuts until golden brown. Add in the minced meat and cook until brown and almost tender. Season with salt, pepper, and cinnamon, then remove from heat and leave to cool. Mix in the cubed tomatoes.

3 Preheat the oven to 400° F (200° C). Roll out the dough on a lightly floured surface to a ¼ in thickness. Cut into 4 in circles. You will need 40 circles in total.

4 Place one level tablespoon of filling in the center of each circle and bring up the edges together at four points to form a square. Pinch the edges together to seal the pies. Arrange on a lightly greased baking tray. Bake for 20 minutes, until golden brown.

Kebab in pastry

Tala kebabi

SERVES 20
COOKING TIME: 2 HOURS

For the dough
2 lb 3 oz all-purpose flour
1 egg
2 Tbsp salt
1 Tbsp white wine vinegar
1 Tbsp butter
1 lb 2 oz margarine

All-purpose flour, to roll out the dough
1 egg yolk, beaten, to brush the pastry

For the filling
3 Tbsp butter
5 medium onions, peeled and finely chopped
2 lb 3 oz lean shoulder or leg of lamb, diced
1 tsp salt
1 Tbsp tomato paste
¾ cup water
1 Tbsp super fine sugar
Pinch of dried mint

1 Start by preparing the dough. Sieve the flour in a bowl and hollow out the center. Break the egg in the hollow and add the salt, vinegar, butter, and 2 tablespoons of the margarine. Mix well and knead until a soft, springy dough is formed. Wrap in a damp cloth and set aside for 15 minutes. Knead again, wrap in a damp cloth, and set aside for another 5 minutes.

2 Roll into an oval shape and place the remaining margarine in the center. Wrap the dough around the margarine and knead again. Roll out to a ¼ in thickness. Fold the edges into the middle and knead once more.

3 Wrap in cling wrap, then in a damp cloth and refrigerate for 2 hours. Then roll out to a rectangle on a floured surface, fold two opposite edges into the center and roll out again. Wrap up in same way and refrigerate for another hour. Repeat the rolling, folding, and refrigerating process once more.

4 To make the filling, melt the butter in a saucepan and gently fry the onions until tender. Add the meat and salt, stir well, then cover, over low heat until the juices evaporate. Then add the tomato paste, water, sugar, and mint, stirring all the time. Lower heat and cook for 15 minutes until the meat is tender. Drain the liquid and set aside. Place the meat in a shallow dish and leave to cool.

5 Preheat the oven to 400° F (200° C). Roll out the dough on a floured surface to a ½ in thick rectangle. Cut into 4 in squares. There should be 40 squares in total. Place one teaspoon of meat filling into the center of each square and fold the edges over to form a parcel. Place the parcels on a baking tray with folded edges underneath and brush with beaten egg yolk. Bake for about 45 minutes or until golden brown.

Rolled borek

Kol boreki

SERVES 10
COOKING TIME: 50 MINUTES

For the meat filling
3 Tbsp butter
1 lb 2 oz lean minced beef
2 medium onions, peeled and finely chopped
1 tsp salt
Pinch of freshly ground black pepper
½ bunch of parsley, finely chopped

For the dough
1 lb 2 oz all-purpose flour
1 egg
½ tsp salt
1½ Tbsp natural yogurt
¾ cup water
9 oz butter

Flour, to roll out the pastry
3 Tbsp butter, melted
2 egg yolks mixed with 1 tsp olive oil, to brush pastry

1 Start by preparing the filling. Heat the butter in a pan and fry the minced meat and onions. Add the salt, stir, and cover. Cook over medium heat for 15 minutes until the liquid has evaporated. Remove from heat, add the pepper and parsley, and set aside to cool.

2 Prepare the dough by sieving the flour in a bowl and hollowing out the center. In the hollow, break the egg and add the salt. Add the yogurt, water, and the unmelted butter. Mix together and knead until a soft, springy dough is formed. Wrap the dough in a damp cloth and cover for 15 minutes.

3 Preheat the oven to 400° F (200° C). Flour a pastry board and roll out the dough very thinly. Brush off any excess flour, then brush the dough with the melted butter. Fold over the lower and upper edges to meet in center and set aside for 15 minutes on a lightly floured surface. Lightly oil the board, then thinly roll out the dough again to form a rectangle that is 3 in wide and as long as the thinness of the dough allows. Sprinkle the filling over the long edge and fold over to form a roll.

4 Grease a baking tray and place the roll of filled pastry, coiling it around itself to form a snail shape. Brush with the egg yolk and olive oil. Bake for approximately 25 minutes or until golden brown.

Borek with eggplant filling

Patlicanli borek

SERVES 6
COOKING TIME: 30 MINUTES

For the filling

2 lb 3 oz eggplants
3 Tbsp olive oil
6 small tomatoes peeled, seeded and diced
7 oz green peppers, seeded and diced
7 oz mixed red and green chilies,
    seeded and diced
2 garlic cloves, peeled and crushed
2 tsp salt
1 Tbsp crushed red pepper flakes
7 oz cilantro and basil,
    combined and chopped
Small bunch of parsley, chopped

For the pastry

12 sheets filo pastry
8½ oz unsalted butter, melted
2 Tbsp butter, for greasing the baking pan
1 egg yolk, lightly beaten, mixed with 1 Tbsp milk
    or cream, for brushing

1 Preheat the oven to 375° F (190° C). Place the eggplants on an oven tray and bake for 10 minutes until they have softened, then set aside to cool. Once cooled, peel the eggplants and mash into a purée with a fork.

2 Heat the olive oil in a pan and fry the tomatoes, peppers, and chilies over medium heat for 5 minutes. Stir in the garlic and eggplant purée, and cook for 2 minutes until soft. Season with salt and pepper flakes, stir in the herbs, and remove from heat.

3 Fold one sheet of filo pastry in four to obtain a rectangle. Brush sparingly with butter and place another folded sheet on top, brushing again with butter.

4 Place one sixth of the eggplant filling in the center of the layered rectangles of pastry. Fold one side over to cover the filling. Brush with butter and fold the other side on top, to create a parcel.

5 Turn the borek parcel upside down and place on a greased baking pan with the folded edges underneath. Make five more parcels in the same way. Brush the parcels with the glaze mixture and bake for approximately 20 minutes, or until golden brown.

Sweet cheese pie

Myzithroboureko

SERVES 6
COOKING TIME: 45 MINUTES

For the filling

1 lb 2 oz myzithra cheese, or any soft
   unsalted cheese
4 eggs, beaten
4 Tbsp super fine sugar
1 Tbsp ground cinnamon

8 sheets of filo pastry
3 Tbsp butter, melted

For the syrup

¾ cup water
3½ oz sugar
Juice of ½ lemon

1   Start by making the filling. In a bowl, mix together the cheese, eggs, sugar, and cinnamon until smooth.

2   Preheat the oven to 350º F (180º C). Prepare the pastry by placing half the filo sheets in a baking pan and greasing the sheets with butter. Spread the cheese mixture on top and cover with the remaining greased sheets.

3   On the pastry, score individual portions with a knife, sprinkle with a little water, and bake for approximately 45 minutes, or until golden brown.

4   To make the syrup, place the water, sugar, and lemon juice in a pan and bring to a boil. Then simmer until the syrup glazes and sticks to the back of a spoon.

5   Place the pastry in a serving dish and serve with the hot syrup.

Borek with spinach filling

Ispanakli tepsi boreki

SERVES 10
COOKING TIME: 50 MINUTES

For the filling
2 lb 3 oz fresh spinach leaves, rinsed,
   drained, and chopped
5 Tbsp olive oil
3 medium-sized onions, peeled and finely chopped
3½ oz kasseri cheese, emmenthal, cantal, or
   gouda, grated
1 tsp salt
1 tsp freshly ground black pepper

For the dough
8½ oz unsalted butter, melted
3 eggs, lightly beaten
3 Tbsp milk
6 sheets filo pastry
Butter, for greasing

1 Start by making the filling. Blanch the spinach leaves in a large pan until wilted. Drain and set aside.

2 Heat the olive oil in a separate pan and fry the onions until brown. Stir in the spinach and sauté for 5 minutes. Add the cheese, salt, and pepper to the pan and return to the heat. Cook for a few seconds, stirring well, then set aside.

3 To prepare the dough, mix the melted butter with the eggs and milk in a bowl. Preheat the oven to 375° F (190° C).

4 Unfold the filo sheets and keep covered under a damp cloth. Taking one sheet at a time, place two sheets on the bottom of a buttered baking tray. Brush each layer of filo with the egg, milk, and butter mixture.

5 Spread the spinach filling over the pastry, then continue layering and brushing the pastry with the egg, milk, and butter mixture until all the pastry is used. Pour the remaining mixture over the top and tuck the edges of the pastry under. Bake for 25 minutes until golden brown.

Thyme pies
Manakish

SERVES 4
COOKING TIME: 20 MINUTES

For the dough
1 lb 5 oz all-purpose flour
¼ oz dry yeast
1¾ cups warm water
Pinch of salt

For the filling
3½ oz dried thyme
2 Tbsp toasted sesame seeds
⅓ cup olive oil

1 Start by preparing the dough. In a large bowl, sieve the flour and hollow the center. Dissolve the yeast in the warm water and add to the bowl with the salt. Knead well until the dough is soft and springy. Cover with a damp cloth and set aside for at least 30 minutes, until the dough has doubled in size.

2 To prepare the filling, mix the thyme with the sesame seeds and olive oil.

3 Preheat the oven to 400° F (200° C). Divide the dough into two equal pieces. Roll out each piece on a lightly floured surface to ½ in thickness, then cut into 4 in circles. You will need 24 circles in total.

4 Press the center of each circle with your fingertips and place 2 level tablespoons of filling in the center and spread out. Arrange on a lightly greased baking tray. Bake for 15 minutes until crispy.

Veiled pilaf

Perdeli pilav

SERVES: 8
COOKING TIME: 1 HOUR 30 MINUTES

1 chicken cut into thighs, legs, and breast halves
1 carrot, peeled and diced
1 medium onion, peeled and finely chopped
Pinch of fresh parsley, chopped
1 bay leaf
4 sheets filo pastry
⅔ cup milk, mixed with 12 Tbsp olive oil

For the pilaf
1 lb 9 oz short-grained rice
1 tsp salt
4 Tbsp olive oil
3½ oz unsalted blanched almonds
  or unsalted pistachios
5½ oz butter
3 tsp super fine sugar
4 cups chicken stock, taken from the
  cooked chicken

1 egg yolk, lightly beaten, mixed with 2 Tbsp olive
  oil, to glaze the pastry

1   Boil the chicken in salted water with the carrot, onion, parsley, and bay leaf for about 15 minutes, or until tender. Remove and discard the chicken bones and skin and cut into small pieces. Strain the stock and reserve for the pilaf.

2   To make the pilaf, rinse and drain the rice, place in a bowl with the salt, and cover with hot water. Allow to stand for 30 minutes, then drain and rinse thoroughly.

3   Heat the olive oil in a pan and fry the nuts until golden brown. Add the butter and when melted add the rice. Stir over medium heat until the rice doesn't stick to a wooden spoon. Stir in the sugar and reserved chicken stock. Bring to a boil, then simmer for 20 minutes. Remove from heat and set aside for 20 minutes. Stir again, then cover and set aside for 10 minutes.

4   Preheat the oven to 400° F (200° C). Lightly grease a baking tray and place the filo sheets one on top of the other, sprinkling the milk and olive oil mixture evenly between them. Let the edges flow over the sides of the tray as you will need them to fold over to cover the top.

5   Tip the pilaf in a neat dome in the center of the pastry and arrange the chicken pieces over the top and sides. Fold the pastry over the rice so it is covered and the edges overlap. Brush the top with the egg and oil glaze. Bake for approximately 35 minutes or until golden brown. Serve hot.

Cheese pastries

Agnopites

SERVES 4
COOKING TIME: 15 MINUTES

For the dough

1 lb 2 oz all-purpose flour
¾ cup water
3 Tbsp olive oil
3 Tbsp lemon juice or raki
Pinch of salt

For the filling

1 lb 2 oz myzithra cheese,
   or any soft unsalted cheese
4 Tbsp milk

Olive oil, for frying
Honey, grape juice syrup, or sugar, to serve

1 Make the dough by mixing together the flour, water, olive oil, lemon juice or raki, and salt. Knead well until a soft, springy dough is formed. Roll out the dough and divide it into small golf ball-sized portions.

2 Prepare the filling by mixing together the cheese and milk until smooth.

3 Make a small hole in each dough ball and fill with 1 teaspoon of the cheese mixture. Pull the dough over to seal the hole and roll the balls into 5 in circles with a rolling pin.

4 Fry the circles in olive oil until golden brown. Serve hot with honey, grape juice syrup, or sugar.

Index